LATIN PRONUNCIATIONS

FOR SINGERS

A Comprehensive Guide to the Classical, Italian, German, English,

French, and Franco-Flemish Pronunciations of Latin

by

Sri Silva

1st edition: 2017©
2nd edition with updated tables: 2020©

ISBN: 978-0-9992554-1-4

Cover photo: Rose Window - Our Lady of Strasbourg Cathedral, France
Cover design: Sandamal P. Silva

TABLE OF CONTENTS

ACKNOWLEDGEMENTS

This book would not be possible without the scholarly work executed by the experts in the field from whom I have quoted throughout. Their work is of immense value to musicology and performance practice. I owe deepest gratitude to all of my music teachers and professors throughout my life, especially Dr. Anthony Lupica, Dr. William Belan, and Don Brinegar, for sharing their wealth of information on music and conducting with me. I thank Jason Bentley for assisting in the proofing of this work. I would like to acknowledge the assistance of music scholar, Patricia Ranum, in so graciously elaborating more fully on the information in her work with me. I thank David Dayan-Rosenman for his assistance in the French translations of passages in Ranum's book.

I thank my family for exposing me to music at such a young age, my colleagues and friends who assisted me in exploring music's infinite possibilities. I am eternally grateful to them for their hard work, interest, support, and dedication.

I thank Joshua Belkin for propelling me to ready this work for publication and his assistance with time management.

PREFACE

Knowledge of proper performance practice is of utmost importance to the modern musician. For many, this includes instrumental timbre, rhythmic articulation, phrasing, and tuning, etc. These factors not only contribute to a composer's style but also to the audiation used when setting music to paper. Absent from this list, however, is an accurate pronunciation of Latin - also of great importance to how a composer hears a text when setting it to music. Although a great percentage of choral music performed by ensembles is in the Latin language, few conductors and singers have more than a surface–level knowledge of the evolutionary and history of the language. This book sets out to elucidate the evolution of the various pronunciations of Latin, and hopes to be a useful tool in performing Latin works with the appropriate corresponding pronunciation. I set out to show that there is no such thing as an "ecclesiastical pronunciation," and that a variety of legitimate pronunciations have been used and can be performed easily by a vocalist or choral ensemble. I have combined the labors of various scholars in the field, including my own, into one easy-to-use handbook in order that the musician may perform works in Latin with the closest pronunciation possible to that which the composer intended. It will be seen. however, that there is disagreement among scholars, and that there are lucanae which may be filled in the futured due to more research or which may be lost to history forever. It will not be possible, at the time of this writing, to perform all works with 100% accuracy and that educated judgements will need to be made by the performer. Nevertheless, it will be seen that the application of the Italian pronunciation to all works in Latin would be a serious blunder. When I began rehearsing the Fauré *Requiem* in the French pronunciation of the composer's time, I observed how the marriage of music and text came to life in a way that the so-called "traditional" Italian pronunciation could not accomplish (e.g., the French phenomenon of final syllable lengthening vs. Italian stress accent). Had Fauré audiated the text in an Italian pronunciation, the text underlay would have been undoubtedly disparate.

Although many pronunciations of Latin are applicable to vocal/choral literature, this book fleshes out six of the most used pronunciations in current choral repertoire: that of the Classical, Italian, German, English, French, and Franco-Flemish. The International Phonetic Alphabet (IPA) is used, as it is the most efficient and understood of all linguistic systems. It would do well for the reader unfamiliar with the IPA to keep a table of symbols handy while reading this book. A number of sources can be found on-line with sound files.

CHAPTER 1: VULGAR LATIN VS. CLASSICAL LATIN: WHICH CAME FIRST?

The use of the Latin language in daily speech can be traced back to the Roman civilization from the eighth century B.C. to the fifth century A.D. Latin, or *Latīna* as it was known to the Romans, developed from groups of Italic languages brought to the Italian peninsula by migrating tribes. It was known as a dialect of those languages and was spoken in Latium, a region around the river Tiber, from which the Roman civilization emerged. It is a common misconception that Classical Latin is the pure and original form of the Latin language. This may be due to the fact that Classical Latin is that form of the language which is most often taught in schools. However, it was Vulgar Latin (from *vulgaris*, meaning "folk") which was the common daily language of the Roman people and of the Empire at large (Palmer 148).[1]

---

[1] "At the death of Augustus in A.D. 14, for example, the estimated population for Italy was 6 million and for the other predominantly Latin–speaking provinces of the West it was some 20 million" (Pulgram 158: 309 qtd. in Sampson 42).

Direct sources for a clear Vulgar pronunciation have been lost to history since it was primarily a spoken language.[2] Linguists formulate theories based on the Romance languages which it birthed. Knowledge of Vulgar Latin pronunciation, then, is a reformulation — a working backwards — from the Romance languages and is a topic subject to much debate. Furthermore, there is debate on what Classical and Vulgar Latins even are. Some scholars see Vulgar Latin as a corruption of Classical Latin (Dégert). Others maintain that Classical Latin survived into the middle ages and became Medieval Latin (Rigg 6). Others indicate that the term "Classical" refers to a genre representative of a few ancient authors such as Cicero and Virgil (Citroni). For purposes of research, comparison, and contrast, Classical Latin (whose pronunciation we know) will be used as a point of departure in discussing pronunciation variants, as the pronunciation of Vulgar Latin, if different, cannot be clearly determined.

According to Antoine Dégert in "Ecclesiastical Latin," Classical Latin was a language form developed by and for the educated and sophisticated upper classes of the Roman Empire. Furthermore, it was formulated based on the syntax, vocabulary, and pronunciation of Classical Greek — highly regarded by educated Romans (Palmer 96). He states,

> Originally the Roman people spoke the old tongue of Latium known as *prisca latinitas* [old Latin]. In the third century B.C., Ennius and a few other writers trained in the school of the Greeks undertook to enrich the language with Greek embellishments. This attempt was encouraged by the cultured classes in

---

[2] "With regard to pronunciation, we know that significant accent differences existed even at the period of the greatest regional and social cohesion. Thus, Cicero (106–43 B.C.) remarks specifically on differences of intonation and sound quality as the distinguishing features of the orators of Cisalpine Gaul...and elsewhere censures the 'thick and foreign' quality of the speech of the then fashionable Cordovan poets" (Sampson 42).

Rome, and it was to these classes that henceforth the poets, orators, historians, and literary coteries of Rome addressed themselves. Under the combined influence of this political and intellectual aristocracy was developed that classical Latin which has been preserved for us in greatest purity in the works of Caesar and of Cicero.

Classical Latin was primarily a literary language. Used on monuments, in government and legal documents, poetry, and prose, Classical Latin was largely disjunct from the average Roman's daily life. It may or may not have been spoken by the upper classes, but was, nevertheless, cultivated and learned by them. It can be said that this was a manufactured language, produced by the upper–class society of Rome. With Cicero's passing in 43 B.C., and the duration of Classical Latin literature until around A.D. 100, the era in which this Latin was used barely touches the period in which the earliest Western Latin music was written (Copeman, *Singing in Latin, or, Pronunciation Explor'd* 6).

As the Roman Empire expanded, the Vulgar Latin imposed on the Empire's subjects took on the flavors of the various peoples. According to Harold Copeman, in *Singing in Latin or Pronunciation Explor'd*, "[a]s the Empire grew, Vulgar Latin spread to the colonies with the occupying forces and was commonly learnt by native populations (some of whom ranked as Roman citizens), and was spoken with local accents" (5). The people of the empire differed in ethnicity and language, such as those of the Celtic and Germanic tribes, each with various dialects as well. As Vulgar Latin was embraced by these peoples, changes in pronunciation, syntax, and spelling produced dialects, known today as the Romance languages.

Vocabulary

Differences in vocabulary between the Classical and Vulgar forms of Latin are numerous. The word for "war" in Vulgar is

guerra, whose counterpart in the Classical is *bellum*. Vulgar's
pensare was countered by *cogitare,* "to think," in the Classical. For
"horse," *caballus* was rendered *equus*, and *sera*, "evening," as *vesper*
by the Classicists. One can see the remarkable differences between
the vocabulary of the Classical and Vulgar Latin forms.
Nevertheless, Vulgar Latin continued to evolve; and the chasm
between the Vulgar and Classical forms grew greater in terms of
syntax, grammar, the dissolution of the case system, and, of course,
pronunciation. According to Mason Hammond in *Latin—A
Historical and Linguistic Handbook*:

> Pronunciation was varied and affected by local dialect
> or foreign speech. In short, the spoken Latin of the
> Empire continued to develop, as would any living
> language, while the literary language tended to
> remain faithful to the classical norms, though even in
> it, poetic words were adopted into prose, prepositional
> constructions began to take the place of cases, and
> popular touches appeared. By the end of the third
> century A.D. the gap between the two forms of Latin
> may have been as great as is that between the English
> of Shakespeare's plays and contemporary speech —
> mutually intelligible but still quite different (233).

Pronunciation Differentiations

Although a standard Vulgar Latin pronunciation cannot be
determined, information can be gleaned from comparison to
Classical Latin via inscriptions by the uneducated of the Roman
Empire. Epitaphs on tombs of commoners in the Roman Empire,
graffiti, and the *defixiones* or curse tablets — used to ask the gods to
inflict punishment on others — give evidence of this. One such
defixio is evidence of the differences in spelling (and thus
pronunciation) from Classical: *"Adiuro te demon quicunque es et
demando tibi ex anc ora ex anc die ex oc momento ut equos praisini
et albi crucies occidas, et agitatore Clarum et Felice et Promulum et*

10

Romanum ocidas col!ida neque spiritum illis lerinquas"[3] (Palmer 154). Evident is the spelling of the word "*demon*" which in Classical spelling would have been rendered *dæmon*, where the Æ is pronounced [ai]. Instead, the defixio seems to indicate pronunciation of Vulgar [ɛ]. Also, one can see the loss of H in the words *anc, ora, oc* (Classical *hanc, hora, hoc*). Syntax and case system differences can be seen as well.

Phonemic shifts are also apparent in Vulgar Latin. Intervocalic B shifted to a bilabial fricative [ß] as is seen in spellings of *cuuiculo* for *cubiculo* (similar to Spanish). Reverse spellings are also found: *universis* written as *unibersis, civitatis* as *cibitatis* (Palmer 158). Of course, if Vulgar were the pre–cursor of Classical Latin, it could be stated that Classical Latin organized and systematized the various spellings of Vulgar Latin: –TI– developed into –TY–. Since the second century A.D., this further shifted to –TS– or –TZ– or even simply S: *Vincentia* to *Vincentza, sapientia* to *sapiensia* (158). By the sixth century, evidence of palatization of C is found. According to Palmer, [k] was pronounced wherever C was spelled. Before I and E, [kj] was pronounced, evolving to [tj] and finally [ts] as well as [tʃ] (158).

Spelling

The Classical Latin alphabet used 22 characters: A, B, C, D, E, F, G, H, I, K, L, M, N, O, P, Q, R, S, T, V, X, and Z. The Latin script derived from an alphabet which was in use by Dorian Greeks in the region of Campania (Peck 12). The letters K and Z became nearly obsolete at a very early time in Latin spelling. K continued to be used for Kalendæ (the first day of the month) and K.K. as an abbreviation for the legal term *calumniæ causa*, among other words. However, the original use of the letter C was for the phoneme G.

---

[3] De 8753, DV 861. Translated by Palmer as "I adjure thee demon, whosoever thou art, and demand of thee that from this hour, this day, this moment, thou afflict and kill the horses of the green and white (faction) and kill and batter the driver Clarus and Felix and Primulus and Romanus and leave no breath of life in them."

When K fell into disuse, C took its place. C was then slightly modified to the letter G about the year 230 B.C. Around A.D. 44, the letter Y was used to depict the Greek *v,* pronounced [y]. Double consonants were not written as such until about the second century B.C., in imitation of Greek usage. Furthermore, long and short vowels were depicted with a variety of tools. The first was to double the vowel (as in Dutch), e.g., *votum* written as *vootum.* A second method was to use the circumflex to mark the long vowel. Another method was to visually make the letter larger than the others: DICO, while another was to add an E: PUEREI (instead of *pueri*).

Quantity and Stress

Accent, or syllabic stress, was a distinguishing feature between the Classical and Vulgar Latins. According to Palmer, accent is " . . . the prominence given by various means to one syllable of a word over others of the same word or utterance" (211). He states that the accent can be produced in languages in either of two ways: " . . . by pronouncing at a higher pitch . . . or by a stronger expulsion of breath (the stress . . . accent)" (211). Palmer explains that Latin grammarians are not in agreement as to which of the above two methods of word stress were used in Classical Latin (211). He continues to mention that the view held by most French linguists is that the "pitch accent persisted down to the fourth century A.D." (211). A number of works written by the Classical poets who based their rhythms on the quantity of syllables rather than stress are evidence of this (211). However, in everyday speech (i.e., Vulgar Latin), the opposite was true and the stress accent was used.

According to Peter Boyd-Bowman, one of the effects of stress accent in Vulgar Latin was the phenomenon of syncope — the dropping of a syllable or sound in pronunciation (1). Thus, *domina,* "lady," evolved to *domna* which further evolved to Italian *donna.* The same is true for *dominus,* "lord," which evolved to *domnus,* then modern French *dom* and Spanish and Portuguese *don.* As Vulgar Latin continued to evolve, changes in the place of accentuation evolved as well. Classical words like *pariĕtem* caused the I to become consonantal and hence the accent was transferred to the following syllable: *caryétem* (Palmer 155). Furthermore, penultimate vowels before a consonant group ending in –R shifted the accent to the penultimate: *ténebræ* then became *tenébræ*; *íntegrum* became *intégrum*.

It is necessary to take a moment to discuss the differences between the long and short vowel and the long and short syllable. Long and short vowels are an element of the articulation of phonemes, as listed in the table below. Long and short syllables are an element of the length of time taken to pronounce a syllable. The short syllable was taken as a unit of length and the long syllable as two units of length which would be pronounced twice as long (*The Teaching of Classics* 213). A short syllable is one that contains a short vowel followed by one or no consonants. A long syllable is one that contains either a long vowel, or a short vowel followed by two or more consonants (with the exception of QU and mute and liquid consonants). The rules of long and short syllables, also called "quantity," has only to do with verse and rhythmical prose and not in reciting prose, the practice of oratory, and nothing at all with ordinary speech (213–214).

Nasals

Latin's use of nasal vowels is also evident in Classical pronunciation. Even spellings reflected this. (Nasal orthography will be discussed more in the chapter on French Latin). The letter N was often omitted; and where it was used orthographically, it was a marker of nasalization (Allen 28). Words like *consul* and *censor* were spelled in very early times without the N (i.e., *cosol, cesor*) (28). Even Cicero is known 'not to have pronounced' N in many words (28). This similar phenomenon occurs with M where it, when occurring in final–syllable position, is not counted as a syllable. This is one of the rules of Classical poetry. Allen states that this can be assumed to be nasalization (29).[4] For example, *multum ille* is a three–syllable phrase where –M is a sign of nasalization (Gibbs). One can now see easily the evolution of *amicum* to *amigo* in Spanish. Elision of final –M occurred in all Romance languages for all words except monosyllables, e.g., French *rien* from *rem* (Ward 274). Vowel nasality in Latin will be discussed further in the chapter on French Latin.

The pronunciation of Classical Latin has been the subject of humanist scholars and linguists since the Renaissance. It is because of this that in the nineteenth century, when Classical Latin pronunciation was beginning to be adopted by schools in England, it came to be called the "Reformed" or "Restored" pronunciation of Latin: a reform of the English pronunciation of Latin used at the time. Its purpose of being instituted in British schools was subject to much debate, so much that the Incorporated Association of Assistant Masters in Secondary Schools argued that "carelessness in pronunciation inevitably leads to false quantities, and misspellings which in turn lead to mistranslations" (*Teaching of Classics* 31). Although the use of this "Restored" pronunciation was gaining ground in the United States, Scotland, and England, it was only finally adopted by academic conferences in England in 1906 (210).

---

[4] "It is generally assumed that in Classical Latin there were no nasal vowel phonemes . . . However, there are grounds for believing that strongly nasal vowels arose at various stages in the history of Latin including the Golden Age period and that phonemically nasal vowels may even have become established in some varieties of Latin. This is indicated by the fact that certain phonological changes have operated which seem to imply heightened vowel nasality. All the changes involve the weakening and sometimes the deletion of nasal consonants appearing in syllable–coda position" (Sampson 42–43).

Table 1: Classical Latin Pronunciation[5]

Vowels			
A	a: (short)	[ə]	
	ā (long)	[a]	
E	e (short)	[ɛ]	
	ē (long)	[e]	
I	i (short)	[I]	
	ī (long)	[i]	
O	o (short)	[ɔ]	
	ō (long)	[o]	
U	u (short)	[ʊ]	
	ū (long)	[u]	
Y	y (short)	[Y]	
	y (long)	[y]	
Diphthongs			
Æ		[aI]	
AU		[aʊ]	
EI		[eI]	
EU		[ju]	
Œ		[oI]	
UI		[wi]	
Consonants		All double consonants are pronounced doubly.	
B		[b]	
BS		[ps]	e.g., *urbs*
BT		[pt]	e.g., *obtinēre*
C		[k]	

[5] Copeman suggests Classical Latin pronunciation for the *Oedipus rex* of Stravinsky (a work translated from French into Latin) since it uses K for C (*Singing in Latin or Pronunciation Explor'd* 230) and the music of C. V. Stanford since he was a student at Trinity College when Cambridge began to implement this pronunciation (199, 202).

D		[d]	D was non–dental (Lindsay 80). When the next word begins with a vowel: [t] (*The Teaching of Classics* 212).
CH		[k]	
G		[g]	
GN		[gn]	(Lindsay 64)
		[n]	(*The Teaching of Classics* 212)
H		[h]	
J/I		[j]	
K		[k]	
M		[m]	But mute or as a nasal vowel before an initial vowel or H in the following word (Lindsay 67)
NC/NQU		[ŋ]	(*The Teaching of Classics* 212)
NG		[ŋ]	(Palmer 227 and Lindsay 65)
		[ŋg]	(*The Teaching of Classics* 212)
NS		The N was mute	e.g., *consul* was pronounced "cosul". It is not certain whether N was a sign of vowel nasalization (*The Teaching of Classics* 212).
P		[p]	
PH		[pʰ]	i.e., aspirated
R		[ɾ] or [r]	According to the Incorporated Association of Assistant Masters in Secondary Schools, always trilled whether at beginning, middle, or end of words (212)
S		[s]	
SC		[sk]	

16

T		[t]	T was non–dental (Lindsay 80)
TH		[tʰ]	i.e., aspirated
U	When unaccented, preceded by Q, sometimes S, and sometimes G, and followed by a vowel	[w]	e.g., *quia* = [kwia]; *suāvis* = [swa–]; but not in *suōrum* = [suo–]
V		[w]	
X		[ks]	
Z		[dz]	
		[zd]	Used when corresponding to the Greek ζ (*The Teaching of Classics* 211)

Source: John C. Trautman, *The Bantam New College Latin and English Dictionary*. New York: Bantam (1995): 4–5 except where otherwise indicated.

CHAPTER 2: HOW LATIN PRONUNCIATION MULTIPLIED AND CONVERGED

Medieval Latin

From the first days of its imposition by the Romans, the European peoples began to pronounce Latin with their own speech patterns (Rigg 6). Thus, did it evolve into the various Romance languages and dialects used from Medieval times to the present day. Yet a formal, universal Latin was well–utilized throughout the medieval era in universities, scholarly writings, the translation of the Bible (from Hebrew and *Koine* Greek), and the rites and prayers of the Catholic Church. Latin continued to be used in the courts of kings, in civil and church law, and in scientific writings on agriculture and medicine (Hammond 235, 238). Its vocabulary, as with any language, adapted to the field or profession which used it (237). According to Mason Hammond, "Pronunciation was varied and affected by local dialect or foreign speech. In short, the spoken Latin of the Empire continued to develop . . . " (233). This is what today is termed "Medieval Latin." It was used from around the fourth century to the year 900 when Romance languages (formerly Latin dialects) began to be legitimized by being written down.

Disagreement ensues on whether Medieval Latin is Vulgar or

Classical. A. G. Rigg, for instance, claims that Medieval Latin is ". . . simply Classical Latin, the language of Roman civilization 100 B.C. to A.D. 100, as learned and practiced in the Middle Ages, though somewhat modified" (6). However, did the Latin of the Middle Ages sound like the Latin of Virgil and Cicero? Clear departures of form, syntax, and vocabulary can be seen from the Medieval writings. Joseph Farrell questions whether a clear departure from Classical Latin can be determined at all, while noting that after the third century, when no further Classical works were written, the nostalgic codification of Classical Latin by grammarians marks the death of a body of work. Nevertheless, the continuity of Latin, utilized in many aspects of life throughout the Middle Ages can be termed "Medieval Latin."

Ecclesiastical Latin

Although much of the Roman Empire, at the time of its decline in the fifth century A.D., was very familiar with Greek, many of the inhabitants of the city of Rome were bilingual in Greek and Latin (Palmer 186), and liturgies may have taken place in both languages. In the fourth century, a shift towards a Latin liturgy begins to take place. According to *History of the Sung Liturgy*:

> In the beginning there was no thought of a liturgical language. The prayers of the liturgy were said in the vernacular . . . which originally was Greek or Aramaic. We are not certain when the language of the Roman liturgy became Latin. Most authorities agree that probably both Latin and Greek were used for some time, and that about the fourth century Latin began definitely to supplant the Greek in liturgical use (Marietta 89).

Yet, evidence of Latin use in the Church can be traced back even further, to the year A.D. 180 (the death of Marcus Aurelius). With the composition of the *Acts of the Martyrs of Scillium*, the first Christian text known to be written, the death of several martyrs refusing to offer sacrifice on behalf of the emperor was documented (Farrell 9). This occurred in Scillium, near Carthage. Concurrently, the first Latin translations of the Bible were being made. What is interesting to note is that the shift to Latin in the Church occurred not at Rome but in Africa. According to the Catholic Encyclopedia, "various local Churches must have seen the necessity of rendering into Latin the texts of the Old and New Testaments, the reading of which formed a main portion of the Liturgy. This necessity arose as soon as the Latin speaking faithful became numerous, and in all likelihood it was felt first in Africa" (Dégert).

The early Church Father, Tertullian (A.D. 160–220), caused the Church in Africa to begin to feel the pull of the Latin language, for he "has been rightly styled the creator of the language of the Church" (Dégert). Following the *Acts of the Martyrs of Scillium* and the early Latin translations of the Bible, Tertullian's writings are of great importance within the corpus of the earliest Christian Latin texts. Born in Carthage, he studied law, converted to Christianity, and was ordained a priest. Known as the Father of Ecclesiastical Latin, Tertullian borrowed from Greek what the Latin of the time could not express. According to Palmer, "The infinitely flexible Greek proved adequate not only to tell in simple language the moving story of the Saviour and His Passion; it had also rapidly furnished a rich technical language for the organization and the doctrinal formulation of the Church" (184). New words such as "*baptisma*," "*ecclesia*," "*martyr*," "*Paracletus*," were borrowed from Greek, while the following legal terms from Classical Latin were given theological meanings: "*sacramentum*," "*peccator*," "*gratia*" (Dégert). Tertullian coined more than eight hundred fifty of these neologisms which gave verbal expression to Christian theology. In essence, Tertullian provided Christianity with its own Latin vocabulary: "Ecclesiastical Latin."

This new Ecclesiastical Latin paved the way for St. Jerome's Vulgate of the fourth century — the first complete Latin translation of the Bible. St. Jerome developed three hundred fifty new words, and his Vulgate formed the capstone for Ecclesiastical Latin language on the whole (Dégert). St. Jerome, being a Classicist, adopted much of his Biblical vocabulary from the Classical Latin of Cicero (Dégert). Thus, what is referred to as "Ecclesiastical Latin" is not a type of pronunciation, but a set of vocabulary — an ecclesiastical jargon. Referring to Latin as *ecclesiastical*, then, is a classification of a lexicon such as *medical* Latin, *botanical* Latin, and *legal* Latin.

Chant

The first Christian hymns to be composed in the new Ecclesiastical Latin introduced by Tertullian, were written in the fourth century by St. Ambrose, bishop of Milan. It is difficult to determine which accent was used in these Milanese hymns and in Gregorian chant. Chant scholar, Willi Apel, shows how St. Ambrose even uses Classical quantitative syllabification, such as four iambic feet per line. The hymn, *Véni redémptor géntium*, is one example:

> *Vení redémptor géntiúm*
> *Osténde pártum vírginís*
> *Mirétur ómne séculum*
> *Talís decét partús Deúm.* (qtd. in Apel 423)

Obvious are the deviations from word accent (syllabic stress) in favor of the long and short quantities of Classical poetry. The odd placement of accent marks in the above example shows Classical quantities of long vowels. In accentual meter, the first syllable should be accented in *Véni*, as well as the first syllable of every word in the last line (424).

However, Martin R. P. McGuire argues, in "The Pronunciation of Latin: Its History and Practical Problems," that Classical pronunciation only applies to literature from 150 B.C. to A.D. 200, adding that by the end of the second century A.D. divergences from Classical pronunciation were already occurring (77). He states:

The Liturgy of the Church contains elements that range from the second century of our era to the present time, and many of these elements entered the Liturgy when Latin was being pronounced in a manner quite different from the Classical. I have in mind, of course, the considerable body of liturgical texts composed in Latin Antiquity and in the Middle Ages. In actual fact, Latin pronunciation was no longer Classical in any strict sense when the earliest Latin liturgical texts were being composed. The Church has really never had a uniform, unchanging pronunciation of Latin throughout its long history, nor could this have been possible. Hence, any pronunciation that it adopts for the sake of uniformity must be arbitrary because it must be applied to texts composed at dates as much as eighteen hundred years apart. . . . A vernacular pronunciation of Latin based on the pronunciation of one of the Romance languages is clearly the best solution, and Italian has most in its favor. (79–80)

First Reform by Charlemagne

Despite the continued erosion of the Roman Empire by barbarian invasions in the 5th century, Christianization of the barbarians ensued, primarily due to monasticism under St. Benedict and the French bishops (Copeman, *Singing in Latin, or, Pronunciation Explor'd* 6). However, in the northern–most parts of the empire, the Germanic dialects (which became the languages of German, Dutch, English, and Scottish) continued to be spoken. Nevertheless, Latin was used in the liturgies and was pronounced "with the local habits of speech" (6).

The varying pronunciations were not regulated until the 8th century under Charlemagne, an emperoro who had a zealous interest in the education of his subjects, yet was himself illiterate. He petitioned Alcuin, a deacon of York, to assist him in the ecclesiastical and educational reform of what would eventually be called the Holy Roman Empire. With the assistance of Alcuin, Charlemagne was then able to initiate a campaign to reform the "Latin" being spoken in the empire to a Classical ideal. Latin was nearly unrecognizable in comparison to its earlier forms since it had already been developing into dialects. Priests' sermons were no longer being understood in Latin, and they eventually reverted to preaching in the local dialects (7).

Copeman states that the pronunciation of the Latin spoken in the Middle Ages began to show some differences from the Classical. Citing the 13th-century sequence, the *Dies iræ*, He comments that the Classical diphthong Æ evolved to the monophthong [ɛ] (7):

> *Recordáre, Jésu píe*
> *Quod sum cáusa túæ víæ*
> *Ne me pérdas ílla díe.* (*Liber Usuális* 1811)

However, as seen previously in the defixio example, this was already a feature of Vulgar Latin.

Second Wave of Reforms: Renaissance and Post–Renaissance Scholars

A vast number of linguistic scholars from the 15th through the 20th centuries either complained of or praised the state of pronunciation variants in their time. They can be divided into two groups: humanists, who desired to revert to a Classical pronunciation of Latin, and nationalists, who defended the use of their regional pronunciation as authentic and the most legitimate. The humanists complained that the Latin spoken by foreigners could not be understood, while nationalists praised their own pronunciation, doing so on nationalistic or patriotic grounds, seeing their own pronunciation as the most authentic. The humanists documented, often in a jocular manner, the speech habits of those who spoke "incorrectly." Their ridicule of other pronunciations provides us with documented evidence of what these pronunciations sounded like. However, according to Ross Duffin, three problems exist when trying to encapsulate the pronunciation of a certain time or country. These are: (1) the non–standardization of pronunciation within a given country; (2) the ability of the authors to write about the pronunciation of another country, using their own language as a model; and (3) the extent to which singers were influenced by either the humanist reforms or their national pronunciation during the time of documentation (217). Although the analysis of all texts of all Renaissance and post–Renaissance scholars would significantly surpass the compass of this book, a list has been included in Appendix B of all known documented historical works regarding Latin pronunciation variants.

Desiderius Erasmus (1466/69–1536) is of primary importance in the documentation of pronunciation variants. In his *De recta Latini Græcique sermonis pronuntiatione* of 1528, Erasmus uses a bear and a lion as characters in dialogue with each other. They speak of the correct and incorrect ways of pronouncing Latin. In one anecdote, Erasmus complains of the fact that neither a Frenchman nor a German could be understood well, when speaking Latin to an emperor whom they were welcoming. When the Frenchman gave his speech, the Italians thought him to be speaking French. All began to laugh. The Frenchman, who was well put off, then stumbled upon some phrases. After finishing his speech, all in the room thought someone must recover the situation. They pushed forward a German doctor to speak next. When he got up to speak, his Latin was so aspirated — in Germanic fashion — that the laughter grew even worse (472).[6] While Erasmus stipulates what he considers to be a proper pronunciation of Latin in the Classical style, we are able to glean from his work what some of the Italian, German, English, and French pronunciations of Latin sounded like, as well. These will be enumerated in the respective chapters to follow.

---

[6] The full text of this story can be found in Appendix A.

John Hart published *An Orthography* in 1569. He was interested primarily in spelling reform of the English language at the time (Copeman, *Singing in Latin, or, Pronunciation Explor'd* 81). Hart was a contemporary of Shepherd, Tallis, and Byrd whose use of English Latin pronunciation we can understand through *An Orthography*. Hart's text not only discusses English, but also the Latin pronunciations used in Italy, Germany, England, and France, among other several countries. Among his various discussions on vowels and consonants, he defends the use of the diphthong [əI] for I on accented syllables in English Latin. He also speaks of consonantal I sounding as [dʒ].

William Bullokar (b. 1530), a teacher from Sussex, was another figure interested in spelling reform. In his 1580 *Booke at large,* Bullokar devised a new system of English orthography only a few years after Hart (Copeman, *Singing in Latin, or, Pronunciation Explor'd* 93). He discusses the use of Latin in England at the time. Among his several descriptions of consonants and vowels, he states that the Latin C has two sounds as ". . . alway the sound of k, except :e: or :i: followe it in the same sillable...[where] it hath alway the sound agréeing to the sounds of his olde name (seé) nere agréeing to the sounde of :s:" (qtd. in Copeman, *Singing in Latin, or, Pronunciation Explor'd* 94). He mentions that Latin E has two sounds as well: [ɛ] and [I] (93). Bullokar also describes the sound of consonantal I in the same manner as Hart.

Justus Lipsius (1547–1606) of Brabant (partly modern–day France) was a student of the Jesuits in Cologne. A Protestant, he nevertheless taught at the Catholic University of Louvain after having lived in Rome for two years as Latin secretary to a cardinal. When asked to write a "true" Latin pronunciation, he produced in 1586 *De recta pronunciate latinæ linguæ dialogus*. Lipsius defends Classical pronunciation, while giving evidence of the errors of contemporary Latin. He complains that no one distinguishes quantity anymore between long and short vowels. He points out the necessity to differentiate between *mālum* (apple tree) and *malum* (bad man), as well as "*Anum ebraim ab Ano obsceno*," i.e, "a drunk old woman from a filthy anus" (with a long A in *ano*, i.e., āno) (qtd. in Copeman, *Singing in Latin, or, Pronunciation Explor'd* 98).

Robert Robinson, published a linguistic treatise, *The Art of Pronuntiation* [sic], in 1617. In his preface, he complains that although Hebrew, Greek, and Latin were printed consistently

> . . . yet in utterance of them in speech, they are so diversly pronounced, that men of different nations (though therein very learned) cannot one suddenly understand the other, or conference had betweene them in any of those languages, every one of them inclining to the manner of pronunciation of their owne country speech. (qtd. in Copeman, *Singing in Latin, or, Pronunciation Explor'd* 104)

He also distinguishes between long and short vowels in Classical style. His descriptions of the Latin used in England at the time show the precursor of "Old Style Latin" (which will be enumerated further in chapter 5), where the still current pronunciation of *habeas corpus* is used, as well as the Anglican Church's [vInajti] for *venite*.

Christoph Bernhard (1628–1692) of Danzig was entrusted by Heinrich Schütz with the vocal training of the choirboys of the Dresden Court. In Bernhard's book on proper singing, *Von der Singe–Kunst oder Manier*, he elaborates upon rules of Latin pronunciation. Bernhard states that one should not speak in dialects, but in the most formal style of his country's language (*Meissnich* for Germans, Roman and/or Florentine for Italians). Although he defends the singer's own national pronunciation of Latin, he asserts that if a singer were to pronounce Latin in the Italian way, ". . . as indeed most singers are wont to do, I would judge this not only admissible but also right and prudent, for weighty reasons (which cannot be spelled out here)" (qtd. in Copeman, *Singing in Latin, or, Pronunciation Explor'd* 106). Bernhard's criticism of contemporary Latin pronunciation in Germany is very telling. He warns against the confusion between B and P, D and T, and F and V, and recommends not pronouncing ST, SP, and SC with initial [ʃ].

Dom Jacques Le Clerc was an eighteenth–century Benedictine monk of France. His manuscript on French Latin pronunciation was discovered in the Bibliothèque Nationale de Paris by French music scholar, Patricia Ranum who published the document in 1991 in her *Methode de la prononciation latine dite vulgaire ou a la francaise: Petite methode a l'usage des chanteurs et des recitants d'apres le manuscrit de dom Le Clerc.*[7] Le Clerc defends the use of Latin in the French style on nationalistic grounds. He argues, ". . . the Italian pronunciation of Latin cannot set the rule for Latin, as Latin is quite changed by it. . . . All the people who learn to speak Latin, except the French, pronounce Latin [U as] *ou,* as do the Italians, Spanish, Germans, Polish, English, etc., who mock us for the way we pronounce it" (qtd. in Ranum 20).

Further Evidence

In addition to the above scholars, further evidence of regional pronunciation variants comes from the following types of documentations: alliteration and rhymes, spellings, loan words, and comparative philological developments (Rigg 47). The 14th-century English hermit, Richard Rolle, uses heavy English Latin alliteration in his *Melos Amoris.* This piece of literature illustrates how C and SC before front vowels were pronounced [s]; while IU at the beginning of a word was pronounced [dʒ]:

> *sanctus secernitur a seculi singultu et singular*
> *solacium*
> *scilicet celeste sumit incessantur*
> *iuvenis iusticiam iuravi gestare genusque iudicii*
> *per omne habere* (qtd. in Rigg 47)

---

[7] Le Clerc's rules for French Latin remarkably match the findings in Copeman's *Singing in Latin, or, Pronunciation Explor'd* based on different sources.

Rhymes such as *"Requiescant in pace"* with *"Hé, qui est–ce?–Quentin.–Passez!"* in French literature give further indication of the nature of pronunciation variants (Ewart and Marouzeau qtd. in Brittain 32).

Spelling confusion shows evidence of pronunciation variants. One of the differences from Classical Latin is the use of E for Œ and Æ, and CI instead of TI. The *Deo gracias!* of the fifteenth–century carol "Adam Lay Ybounden" also illustrates the latter. The loss of written H is apparent in medieval spellings, as in *abet* rather than Classical *habet* (Rigg 48). The use of NGN for GN as in *angnus* [aŋgnʊs] and *dingnus* [diŋgnʊs] is also a feature of English [and French] Latins (Rigg 48).

Loan words from Latin indicate the pronunciation at the time of borrowing (48). Therefore, the [dʒ] sound for initial IU– and G– are evidenced by "judicial" and "germinate" which come from Latin words *iudicium* and *germen*. The English word "verbal" indicates that [v] and not Classical [w] was obtained from Latin *verbum*. In French, the manner in which *temptation* is pronounced indicates the cognate in Latin was pronounced with nasal vowels and silent P. John Hart gives evidence of this in his phonetic transcription of the *Pater Noster*, as he heard it in the sixteenth century (Copeman, "French Latin" 91).

Comparative philological developments are of considerable import to both Old Style English and Tudor pronunciations of Latin. The phenomenon of the Great Vowel Shift, beginning in the fifteenth century, caused vowels to rise in the mouth as well as the development of diphthongs. This manifestation was mirrored in the pronunciation of Latin in England at the time (Rigg 48). When the English word "time," previously pronounced [tim], was evolving toward modern [taɪm], it can be seen how "Dei" was Anglicized to [diai]. Robert Robinson documents that Latin *calor* was pronounced as the Middle English *labor*, where A is pronounced [æ] (Rigg 48).

28

How Italian Pronunciation Became the Norm

On November 22, 1903, Pope St. Pius X promulgated the *motu proprio, Tra le sollecitudine.* With this document, he gave instructions and guidelines regarding the use of sacred music in the liturgies of the Roman Rite. Pius desired to return to the ancient chant tradition of the Church and, by doing so, encourage lay participation in the singing of liturgies. At this time, showy, concerted Mass and Office settings from the seventeenth through nineteenth centuries were used in the Roman Catholic liturgies (along with works Pius stated "would not be tolerated for a moment even in our second–rate concerts") (Letter to the Cardinal Vicar of Rome). Without discouraging the use of modern compositions, the Pope reiterated the Council of Trent's (1545–1563) admonition against showy music. Trent's support for the revival of Gregorian chant, and the proliferation of polyphony based on the model of Palestrina (*Tra le sollecitudine*).

Since the time of Pius' predecessor, Pope Pius IX, the French monastery of Solesmes had been in charge of a scholarly redaction of the Gregorian chants. Due to the editing of the *Liber Usualis* in 1896 by Dom André Mocquereau, it became evident to the monks that a pronunciation of Latin which preserved the stress accent was much more suitable for the proper rhythmic interpretation of Gregorian chant. In 1903, with the republication of the *Liber Usualis*, a table was included for the "correct" pronunciation of Latin. Solesmes further included "les règles de la prononciation romaine du latin" in their Gregorian chant manuals (Brittain 40). This was the first attempt by the Church to reign in the various pronunciations. In a 1912 letter to the Archbishop of Bourges, Pope St. Pius X states,

> The question of the pronunciation of Latin is closely bound up with that of the restoration of the Gregorian Chant. . . . The accent and pronunciation of Latin had great influence on the melodic and rhythmic formation of the Gregorian phrase and consequently it

is important that these melodies should be rendered in the same manner in which they were artistically conceived at their first beginning. (qtd. in De Angelis 4)

Nationalistic ties to pronunciation grew strong and resistance fomented. The aged philologist and monk, Abbot Rousselot, wrote in 1928:

Love Latin in the guise which its centuries with us have given it, fitting it to the growth of our language: because it has never ceased to be ours. Don't force it to take up a foreign or harlequin disguise that would distance it from us, and which would produce, in the French language if it adopted such a disguise, blemishes which hurt our ears, a lasting embarrassment for our eyes. (qtd. in Copeman, *Singing in Latin, or, Pronunciation Explor'd* 211)

Msgr. Moissenet, a French priest and organist, not only wrote a book supporting the French pronunciation of Latin (*La prononciation du latin*) in 1928, he even founded (at the age of 80) a magazine called *Bulletin des amis de la prononciation française du latin.* He once snickered, "*A ces règles, évêques et curés veulent croire comme à l'Évangile, parce que les Solesmiens ont parlé. Aveugles eux–mêmes, et à la tête d'autres aveugles, ils ont fait autour d'eux de vraies ténèbres,*" which I have translated as: "These rules, bishops and priests want to believe like they are Gospel, just because Solesmes has spoken. Blind themselves, and at the head of the other blind ones, they have created around themselves true darkness" (qtd. in Brittain 40). In 1972, the German bishops decided to keep the German Latin; however, secular choirs in Germany were already beginning to use the Italian pronunciation (Copeman, *Singing in Latin, or, Pronunciation Explor'd* 12). In 1934, the English linguist Frederick Brittain wrote, "The custom of imitating the Italian pronunciation of Church Latin is unquestionably growing . . . among church choirs and among choral societies. On the Continent,

30

italianization [sic] is by no means universal, even among those who pay ecclesiastical allegiance to Rome" (13).

In England, the switch to Italian pronunciation began somewhat earlier than Pius X's requests. With the rise of the Oxford Movement (1833–1845), the Anglican Church began to revive a medieval Catholic identity in its art, ritual, and dress. Led by Henry Cardinal Newman, among others, Latin was reintroduced into the services. The type spoken in Rome was considered the most "Catholic" (Brittain 67). Newly imported into England, this pronunciation was not readily accepted by hereditary Catholics (those families who had remained Catholic since the Reformation) who did not want a "new" Latin with its "chees and chaws" (67–68).

Some authors (Reeves, and McGuire 77) have claimed that with the issuance of *Tra le sollectitudini* Pius made an official mandate for the Italian pronunciation of Latin in the Catholic Church. However, a reading of the document finds no actual reference to pronunciation. The only documented evidence (thus far) citing the desire for a uniform pronunciation is a personal letter to the Archbishop of Bourges. Thanking him for the implementation of the Roman pronunciation in his diocese, Pius indicates that the issue of pronunciation is tied to the restoration of Gregorian chant (Pius, Letter to Archbishop of Bourges qtd. in De Angelis 4).[8] The other reference to pronunciation is in the *Liber Usualis*, as mentioned above. It cannot be said why no official mandate was made. Perhaps Pius knew how attached the various countries were to their pronunciations. Nevertheless, as it related to regulating sacred music in Catholic liturgies, the Pope supported the cause for a unified pronunciation as was initiated by the efforts of the monks of Solesmes. He referred to this pronunciation as that which is used in Rome (4). Perhaps he knew of the other Italian pronunciations of Latin outside of Rome. Nevertheless, within a span of seventy years, Pius' desires brought practically the whole choral world into a

---

[8] The full text of this letter can be found in Appendix A.

uniform pronunciation of Latin due to his efforts to preserve *Unus cultus, unus cantus, una lingua:* One worship, one chant, one language.

Edits in Choral Repertoire

The choral conductor and singer of early music have much to deal with in regard to published editions. In terms of pronunciation, editions are found having "corrected" the nationalistic spellings of song texts. Rigg states:

> It has been common practice for editors to 'classicize' the texts; that is, to adjust the manuscript spellings to conform more or less to Classical (or more often Schoolbook) Latin. This practice is seen in series such as *Analecta Hymnica*: for the medieval spellings *racio, equs, mechus, celum*, editors often substitute the Classical forms *ratio, æquus, mœchus, cœlum*. This forces Medieval Latin into an alien mold and separates the spelling from its phonetic base. (8)

He further alerts the performer to use the following as a guide for spellings of Æ and Œ: for *præ–, cædo, hæc, quæ, cœlum, obœdire, ratio*, and *retia*, use *pre–, cedo, hec, que, celum, obedire, racio*, and *recia*.

CHAPTER 3: ITALIAN LATIN

What is referred to as the Italian pronunciation by Copeman and Rigg is also referred to as the "Roman" by Pius X. This should not be confused, however, with the Classical pronunciation of ancient Rome. The Italian pronunciation is that which is used in current Roman pronunciation. However, for purposes of clarification, the modern Roman pronunciation will be referenced as "Italian." Rev. Michael de Angelis, author of *The Correct Pronunciation of Latin According to Roman Usage,* distinguishes three types of Latin pronunciation which were used during the Classical Latin period which he dates from 100 B.C. to A.D. 14 (7).[9] These are the tonic, musical, and literary or poetical, consisting of short and long vowels (7). De Angelis states that currently, only the tonic remains. Without distinguishing between a Vulgar and a Classical pronunciation, he does admit that the Latin spoken during the Classical period had varying accents depending on the region of Italy (Greek influence along the coasts, Etruscan in Lazio, and Gallic in upper Italy). In his book, de Angelis states that the Italian pronunciation of Latin does not perfectly preserve the Classical pronunciation. Yet, he goes on to assume that the Latin used during the "golden age" of Classical Latin used in the Roman Empire is

---

[9] A much earlier ending date than that given by Rigg of A.D. 100 (6).

closest to the modern Italian one, which he terms "Roman." De Angelis states:

> One may ask if the Roman pronunciation in actual use corresponds perfectly to the phonetics of the Classic period. We answer, that according to scientific proofs, no one particular class of people has exactly preserved that pronunciation, but, it is safe to conclude that the pronunciation which is closest to it is the Roman, and the one preferred. (6)

If this is not reason enough, then he offers the "motives of discipline and obedience" as sufficient to adopt the Italian pronunciation (6). He further argues that since singers are called upon to sing the praises of God in Latin, "and celebrate by means of the divine art of song, the sublime mysteries of religion, in the same rite, using the same Scriptural texts, the same psalms and prayers that the Holy Mother Church uses in all her Liturgy" that Christians should feel the urgency of this sense of discipline (6).

De Angelis offers three reasons for the similarity of Italian and Classical pronunciations: (1) the Latin language uninterruptedly had its home in Rome for the works of the Church and therefore has never been a dead language and continues to evolve, even coining new words; (2) because scientific proof is lacking for other pronunciations' claims to a direct lineage to the Classical;[10] and (3) Rome is the center of Catholicism and there are too many varied pronunciations. He further necessitates that only one pronunciation is needed so that learned people throughout the world may easily understand one other. De Angelis ends his argument declaring: "*Unus Cultus Unus Cantus Una Lingua*" (7).

The *Liber Usualis* recommends as "vitally important" to Italian pronunciation the "rich, open, warm, sounds of the vowels A

---

[10] De Angelis states that Latin remained unknown outside Italy among the masses, while Latin has been taught grammatically and was cultivated throughout Italy, especially in Rome.

and U" (xxxvi). No exact phonetic symbols are used — only model English words in the English edition. Although the word "Father" is used as a model for the pronunciation of all As, the *Liber* admits that it is difficult to get in English the exact sounds of the Latin vowels, and recommends that the real values of the vowels can "best be learned by ear" (xxxvi). It may be for this reason that Copeman gives IPA [a] for this vowel in his texts since this is the corresponding Italian A. This should also be taken into consideration when using any English text regarding the Italian pronunciation of Latin which does not use the IPA. Of further consideration should be the dental Ds and Ts of Italian pronunciation of which no author comments but are heard in abundance when Italians use this pronunciation of Latin. I have included the pronunciation of these 2 consonants in the table below for ease of reference. For score marking purposes, the IPA diacritic to indicate dentalization may be used as such: [d̪], [t̪].

Copeman states that the pronunciation given in the *Liber Usualis* has a long history and is appropriate for Roman music from the sixteenth century (e.g., Palestrina) to Verdi and onwards (171).[11] However, other regions also had varying pronunciations which will be useful for non–Roman composers (e.g., Vivaldi). Venetian pronunciation can be used up to around 1800. These various Italian pronunciations are shown in the table below compiled from Copeman's *Singing in Latin or Pronunciation Explor'd* 174 and 273–275; his chapter on Italian Latin in *Singing Early Music* 213–215; and from the *Liber Usualis* xxxv–xxxix. Note well that back vowels in Latin are A, O. and U, whereas front vowels are E, Æ, Œ, and I. Double consonants are pronounced doubly except in Venice.

---

[11] It would be appropriate to use Italian pronunciation for the music of Benjamin Britten. In the 1963 recording of his War Requiem conducted by him, the choir and soloist used this pronunciation. Note, however, that when speaking to the musicians, he uses the English pronunciation of Latin.

Table 2: Italian Latin Pronunciation

Vowels			
A		[a]	
	In unaccented syllables in Milan this tends to close toward	[o]	
E/Æ/Œ		[ɛ]	Especially in Tuscany
		[e]	Also used, however the Italian cognate will determine where, e.g., Latin *Deus* = [deus] from Italian *Dio*
	In Venice: before a nasal consonant and in open syllables	[e]	Example of a closed E before a nasal consonant: e.g., *centum* = [seŋtum]
I		[i]	
O		[ɔ]	
		[o]	In some regions depending on Italian cognates, e.g., Latin *suo* = [suo] from Italian *suo*
	In Venice: in open syllables	[o]	
U		[u]	Especially in Florence and Bologna
	In open syllables in the northwest including Mantua but not Parma (but in the Middle Ages as far east as Emilia and Modena)	[y]	
Y		[i]	
Diphthongs			
AI		[ai]	
AU		[au]	
AY		[ai]	
EI		[ɛi]	
EU		[ɛu]	
OU		[ɔu]	

Consonants			
C	Before a back vowel or before a consonant	[k]	
	Before a front vowel		
	- Generally	[tʃ]	
	- In northern Italy except Milan	[ts] or [s]	
	- Possibly in Venice and Mantua	[tj]	
	- In Tuscany (and central Italy possibly) when CI + vowel or CE + vowel	[ʃ]	e.g., *facio* = [faʃo]
	- In Venice until 1700	[ts]	
	- In Venice after 1700	[s]	
	Medially between vowels		
	- In Venice until 1700	[dz]	e.g., *pacem* = [padzem]
	- In Venice after 1700	[z]	
	- In Florence	[ʃ]	
CC		[t:tʃ]	
	In Venice	[z]	Presumably only before front vowels
CH		[k]	
D		[d̪]	i.e., dental
G	Before a back vowel or consonant	[g]	
	Before a front vowel		
	- Generally	[dʒ]	
	- In Rome, the south and northern Italy (except Milan)	[ʒ]	
	- Possibly in the north	[dz]	
	- Possibly in Venice and Mantua	[dj]	
GE	In Venice until 1800	[dz]	

37

GI	In Venice until 1800	[dz] or [j]	
GN		[ɲ]	Prolonged in Tuscany and central Italy
H		Mute	Except in *mihi* (*michi*) and *nihil* (*nichil*) where it is [k]; [ç] in some cities.
J/I		[j]	
	In earlier centuries	[dʒ]	
N + consonant	In Venice	[ŋ]	
R	When with another consonant except in Venice	[r]	i.e., trilled/rolled
		[ɾ]	De Angelis states R is rolled only at the beginning of a word; otherwise, it is flipped
S		[s]	
	Between vowels	[z]	
	Between vowels in the center and the south	[s]	
SC	Before front vowels	[ʃ]	
	Before front vowels in Venice	[s]	
	Otherwise:	[sk]	
SCH		[sk]	
	In earlier centuries	[ʃ]	
T		[t̪]	i.e., dental
TH		[t̪] or [t]	
	In earlier centuries	[ts]	
TI + vowel		[tsi]	Unless preceded by S, X, or T
X		[ks]	
	Between vowels	[gz]	
	In Venice	[z]	

XC	Before front vowels	[kʃ]	
	In Venice	[z]	
Z		[dz]	

CHAPTER 4: GERMAN LATIN

"The Germans (which I am ashamed to vtter) doe howle like Wolves . . . Germany nourisheth many Cantors but few Musicians. For very few, excepting those which are or haue been in the Chappels of Princes, doe truly know the Art of Singing. For those Magistrates to whom this charge is giuen, doe appoint . . . Cantors, whome they choose by the shrilnese of their Voyce . . . thinking that God is pleased with bellowing and braying."
– Ornithoparcus of Central Germany in his *Micrologus* of 1517, translated by John Dowland

Although earlier Roman conquests of the western and southern areas of Germany brought Latin to the area, Latin's real influence in Germany begins in the seventh century when missionaries from the British Isles and northern France arrive. These were St. Columbanus whose mission travelled to St. Gall; St. Kilian who went to the Franks in western Germany; and St. Boniface who converted many in the center and south of Germany (Copeman, *Singing in Latin, or, Pronunciation Explor'd* 166). Subsequently, Charlemagne brought in Alcuin to assist him with ecclesiastical and educational reform. This included the reform of Latin pronunciation. Since it was a learned language in those countries, it was not as corrupt as the Latin spoken in the regions of western Europe whose languages were evolving from Latin. German Latin at this time retained the use of Classical [g] for all Gs primarily in the north. C before front vowels were pronounced [ts]. Both open and closed vowels are used in German Latin. Eventually, Latin in the Germanic regions became shaded by the colors of Germanic speech; and since German dialects were highly regionalized, determining pronunciation remains complex until 1650.

Over time, the German language became standardized, conforming to the one spoken in the Saxon court. The reason: Martin Luther's translation of the Bible into German. This may have created further shifts in the pronunciation of Latin. German pronunciation may have further evolved in the seventeenth and eighteenth centuries due to the fashion for Italian music in the courts of Dresden and Vienna (Copeman and Scherr "German Latin" 259). However, it cannot be determined, as yet, which pronunciation was preferred in these two courts. In the mid–1800s, new "humanists" were trying to reform German Latin. In 1898, with the German *Hochlautung* ("standard pronunciation") one of the important changes was that G was to be [g], or [k] at the end of a syllable, instead of the numerous fricatives used regionally.[12] Educated Latin speech, then, followed the patterns of standardized German. At Fulda in 1947, the Catholic bishops of Germany decided to retain the use of German Latin. In 1972, they decided to continue to use German pronunciation as opposed to the pronunciation of Classical Latin (Copeman, *Singing in Latin, or, Pronunciation Explor'd* 12, 216).

Pope Benedict XVI had tendencies to revert to some German Latin pronunciations. He used closed E on open syllables and [z] for S in initial position. Benedict uses [s] in *Sanctus* of the *Benedicat* (the Blessing), but [z] in *Sancto* of the *Gloria Patri* ("*Pater Noster*

---

[12] The combination of the letters –IG in German is not used in Latin.

with Pope Benedict XVI" and "Papal Blessing", *Youtube*).[13] These are common features of a German pronunciation of Latin.

Syllabification

As in English Latin, where stressed syllables use long vowels and unstressed syllables use short ones, a similar phenomenon occurs in German Latin: in general, closed syllables use open vowels and open syllables use closed vowels. In German Latin up to 1500, double consonants may have been pronounced doubly. After that, they are pronounced singly but still serve the function of indicating that the preceding vowel is open.

The following table is compiled from Copeman, *Singing in Latin or Pronunciation Explor'd* 168–170, 214–221, and Copeman and Scherr, "German Latin" in *Singing Early Music* 261–263. Vowels in IPA separated by a forward slash (i.e., /) are given in "closed"/"open" syllable pairs. This means that the first vowel is used in closed syllables; the second vowel is used in open syllables.[14] If only one is given, then that vowel is used for both types of syllables.

---

[13] The former begins, ". . . *Pater, et Filius, et Spiritus Sanctus* . . ." where the final S of *Spiritus* combines with the initial S of *Sanctus* producing [saŋktʊs]. The latter begins, "*Gloria Patri, et Filio, et Spiritui Sancto* . . ." where the final I of "*Spiritui*" causes the S of *Sancto* to be [z] in German fashion: [zaŋkto].

[14] A closed syllable is one that is "closed" off by one or more consonants. An open syllable is one that is left open by a vowel. For example, the first syllable of *De–us* is open, the second closed. Other terminology includes "blocked" and "unblocked" (Copeman, *Singing in Latin* 20).

Table 3: German Latin Pronunciation

Vowels				
A	Until 1650		[æ] or [ɛ]	Very open like Dutch *aa* in the north. Catholics pronounce *amen* as [ˈɑ:mən]; Protestants as [ɑˈmɛn].
		In the south	[ɔ]	
	1650–Present	Lengthened in accented, open syllables	[a] or [ɑ]	
		In Saxony	[ɔ]	
		For the ending –AS	[əs]	
AO	1650–Present		[o]	Earlier in the period and possibly for the music of Bach
	In current usage		[ao]	
E	Until 1650		[ɛ]/[e]	The former in syllables closed by strong consonants (those not GN, L, or R) or a consonantal group
		In stressed, open syllables in the north	[i]	
		In stressed open syllables in Saxony, Austria, and Bavaria	[ɛ]	

43

		In the center and south, e.g., lower Saxony and Swabia	[eI]	For long E, e.g., *Deus* = [de:IƱs]
		In unstressed open syllables	[e]	e.g., the final E in *deinde* = [dainde]
		In unstressed weak endings	[e]	e.g., *Israel*, *Emanuel*
		Possibly in final position	[ə]	
	1650–Present	In stressed open syllables	[e]	e.g., *miserere* = [mizeˈrerε]
		For *est* and *et*	[est] and [et] respective-ly	
		In all closed syllables and unstressed open syllables	[ε]	e.g., *miserere* = [mizeˈrerε]
Æ	1650–1850		(as E above)	
	1850–Present		[ε]	
EI	Until 1850		[ai]	A diphthong, e.g., *deinde* =[dainde]; similarly: *eia* = [aia]
	In 1700s in Upper Saxony		[e]	
	1850–Present		[εi]	
ES	1650–Present	In final position	[εs]	

EU	1650–Present		[ɔy]	
I	Until 1650	In stressed syllables	[I]/[i]	
		In unstressed syllables	[I]	
		In final position	[i]	
		In the center and south, e.g., Rhineland	[ei] or [ej]	
	1650–Present	In stressed open syllables	[i]	
		In unstressed and all closed syllables	[I]	e.g., *hominis* = [ˈho–mi–nIs]
IS	1650–Present		[Is]	Except *his* = [his]
O	Until 1650	In closed syllables	[ɔ]	
		In unstressed, open syllables	[a]	e.g., *oremus* was pronounced with initial [a–]
		In closed syllables in Western Germany, e.g., Franconia, Frankfurt–am–Main, and Würzburg	[U]	e.g., *noster* was [nUst-]
		In stressed open syllables and monosyllables (e.g., *cor*) in the north, in unstressed open syllables, and in final position	[o]	

	1650–Present		[ɔ]/[o]	
		For long O in Vienna	[ɑ]	
Œ			[e] or [ɛ]	Also as E above. The medieval spelling will usually be with an E. From 1500s–1700s, spellings are usually with Œ, though also with E. In the 1800s, spellings are usually with Æ, i.e., celi/cœli/cæli.
		In Saxony, Austria, and the south	[ɛ]	
			[ø]	Depending on spelling: generally, cœli has been restored to its original spelling of cæli. This pronunciation probably began in the late 1700s. It is used by modern Germans where Œ spellings are used.[15]

---

[15] It is possible that when Œ was beginning to be used more frequently in the 1800s, the pronunciation [ø] began to be used. Mendelssohn's copy of Beethoven's *Mass in D* has red markings bringing down the high notes of the soprano line one octave, possibly indicating that although Beethoven intended [e]

U (also see V below)	Until 1650	In closed syllables and stressed open syllables	[ʊ]	
		In stressed, open syllables and in final position	[u]	
		In stressed, open syllables and in final position in the north	[y]	
	1650– Present		[ʊ]/[u]	
–UR			[ur]	
Y	Until 1800		(as I above)	
	1800s– Present		[y]	
Consonants				
B	Until 1650	In the north	[bʰ]	i.e., aspirated
		In other regions	[p]	Lightly articulated
	1650– Present		[p]	
		Before E, I, O or Y in Saxony	[b]	
C	Until 600		[k]	
	600– Present	Before front vowels	[ts]	
		Otherwise	[k]	

or [ɛ], by Mendelssohn's time/region [ø] was used. The rationale may have been that the latter closed/mixed vowel is difficult for sopranos to sing in the high tessitura (Copeman, *Singing in Latin* 219f).

CC	1650–Present	Before front vowels	[kts]	
		Otherwise	[k]	
CH (for *michi* and *nichil* see below under H)	1650–Present	After A	[x]	
		After a front vowel or consonant	[ç]	
		In initial position or before a consonant	[k]	
D	Until 1650	In the north	[d]	
		In final position and in the center and south	[t]	
	1650–Present	In final position	[t]	
G	Until 1650	In all positions in the south	[g] or [k]	
		In initial position in the north	[x] (or [j] before front vowels)	
		In initial position in Saxony	[ç]	

		In all other regions, as follows:		
		- in final position after a back vowel	[x]	
		- after a back vowel if another vowel follows	[ɣ]	i.e., the voiced equivalent of [x]
		- in final position after a front vowel	[ç]	
		- after a front vowel if another vowel follows	[j]	i.e., voiced palatal fricative, or the voiced equivalent of [ç]
	1650–Present		[g]	
GN	1650–1898		[ŋn]	
	1898–Present		[gn]	
H	1650–Present		[h]	
	Until late 1700s		[ç]	When spelled *michi* and *nichil* (alternative spellings for *mihi* and *nihil* respectively); but CH would be mute in these words in Swabia.
J/I	Until 1650		[j]	
		In the north mainly before front vowels	[g]	

		In Saxony	[ç] or strongly articulated [h]	
	1650–Present		[j]	
P	Until 1650	In the north	[pʰ]	i.e., aspirated
		In other regions	[p]	Lightly articulated
		In Saxony	[p]	Lightly articulated, almost a [b] sound
R	1650–Present		[r]	i.e., rolled/trilled
		In final position	[ɾ]	i.e., flipped, e.g., *pater*
S	Until 1650		[s]	
		In initial position in the north	[z]	
	1650–Present		[s]	
		In initial position before a vowel and between vowels	[z]	Except in compound words e.g., *desuper*, where it is [s]
SC	Until 600		[sk]	
	600–1650	Before front vowels	[ts]	
		Before back vowels and consonants in the northwest and in the music of Heinrich Schütz	[sk]	

		Before back vowels and consonants otherwise	[ʃk]	
	1650–Present	In initial position	[ts]	
		Medially before front vowels	[sts]	
		Otherwise	[sk]	
SCH	Until 1650		[ʃ]	
	1650–Present		[sk]	
SP/ST	Until 1650	In the northwest and in the music of Heinrich Schütz	[sp] and [st]	
		In other regions	[ʃp] and [ʃt]	
	1650–Present		[sp] and [st]	
T			[t]	
		In Saxony	[t]	Lightly articulated, almost a [d] sound except in TI+vowel – see below
TI+vowel			[tsi]	
XC	1650–Present		[ksk]	
		Before front vowels	[ksts]	

51

V	Until 1650		[f]	
		CU/QU/GU/SU (when U + a vowel forms one syllable), the U is treated like a consonant as German V and is as follows:		
		- in the medieval Rhineland	[f]	
		- in Bavaria	[w]	
		- in Saxony	[v]	
	1650– Present		[f] or [v]	
			[v]	CU/QU/GU/SU (when U + a vowel forms one syllable): the U is treated as German V, e.g., *lingua* = [–gva], (but not in *suum* or *quum*)
Z	Until 1650	Possibly in all regions but especially in the southwest	[s]	
	1650– Present		[ts]	
		Also possible, but were considered incorrect	[sd] or [ds]	

CHAPTER 5: ENGLISH LATIN

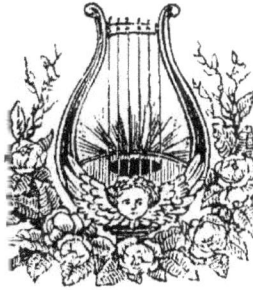

Simple was I and was young;
Kept no gallant tryst, I;
Even from good words held my tongue
Quoniam tu fecisti
—"After Reading Psalms xxxix, xl., etc." Thomas Hardy
(1840-1928)

Latin in Britain goes back to the time of the Roman Conquest of 55 B.C. under Julius Caesar. The original inhabitants of Britain were Celtic (the modern Welsh), and were taught Latin by the Romans themselves. The Celts were driven out of England by several Germanic tribes known as Angles, Saxons, Jutes, and Frisians (Rigg 46). These groups, who eventually became the English, were taught Latin by Catholic missionaries from Ireland, Scotland, and Rome in the sixth century A.D., namely under the patronage of St. Augustine of Canterbury in 597 (46). The pronunciation of this Latin in England is unknown to us.

However, in the late tenth century, Latin pronunciation in England changed due to Norman–French influence. Oswald, archbishop of York, called upon Abbo, an abbot of France, to help him restore the monastic system. After the Norman Conquest in the eleventh century, Latin was taught to the English in an entirely Norman–French pronunciation. Even education was presented in

French until about 1250 when English gradually began to re–emerge. Norman–French pronunciation of Latin was spoken right up to the middle of the fourteenth century. According to Copeman, it is possible that English students still used local pronunciation in trying to imitate their French teachers, while the French were also picking up local English sounds in their daily speech (*Singing in Latin, or, Pronunciation Explor'd* 115). However, Rigg states that from the twelfth and thirteenth centuries it is not discernible whether one should pronounce Latin according to the English Latin style or the style of the Norman French (46). Therefore, he suggests a modified French pronunciation for literature written during the twelfth and thirteenth centuries. He does explain, however, that by the fourteenth and fifteenth centuries one can be fairly certain of an entirely English pronunciation (47). Beginning in the fourteenth century, English came to be the medium of instruction in schools. Latin gradually acquired the flavors of the English language.

The Latin used during the fifteenth and sixteenth centuries is uncertain as well. Also dubbed "Tudor Latin" by Copeman, it was probably a mongrelized Latin, somewhere between Classical and English pronunciations (*Singing in Latin, or, Pronunciation Explor'd* 293). In the sixteenth century, Erasmus tried to revive the Classical pronunciation, the understanding of which was itself obscure at the time, with his book, *De recta Latini Græcique sermonis pronunciatione.* His recommendation to use the Classical pronunciation of Latin was being adopted by scholars in England. It is at this time that English Latin underwent some revisions. It is difficult to determine the exact pronunciation used during this period. It was a tumultuous time due to the Reformation and Henry VIII's three children, the successive monarchs of England: Edward VI mandated that all services were to be in English, Mary Tudor revived Catholic practice (and hence Latin), and Elizabeth I reversed Mary's reforms. Elizabeth did allow for a limited use of Latin in the kingdom, primarily for scholarly purposes. It was continually taught in school and used in law. This English Latin eventually came to be known as "Old Style English Latin" which will be discussed further below.

Rigg provides a general evolution of pronunciation of English Latin from the fifteenth to the seventeenth centuries. Copeman, however, argues that the Tudor Latin and the pure English Latin probably existed side–by–side. Copeman indicates that, in the chanting of the Divine Office and Mass by clergy, the English Latin must have endured, while Tudor Latin would have been used by trained choirs of the day who would have taken up the reforms of Erasmus more readily (293). How choirs would have incorporated the reforms of Erasmus may not have been consistent, however. Copeman indicates that a variety of pronunciations existed among Tudor choirs.

The following chart is compiled from information found in Copeman's *Singing in Latin, or, Pronunciation Explor'd* 111–134, 194–203, 283–284, and Rigg's "Anglo–Latin" in *Singing Early Music* 50–55. From the years 800–1066 double consonants are pronounced doubly (Copeman, *Singing in Latin, or, Pronunciation Explor'd* 115). The sounds for Old Style English Latin will need to be further guided by Sargeaunt's rules discussed below. Vowels in IPA separated by a forward slash (i.e., /) are given in "closed"/"open" syllable pairs. This means that the first vowel is used in closed syllables; the second vowel is used in open syllables.[16] If only one is given, then that vowel is used for both types of syllables.

---

[16] A closed syllable is one that is "closed" off by one or more consonants. An open syllable is one that is left open by a vowel. For example, the first syllable of *De–us* is open, the second closed. Other terminology includes "blocked" and "unblocked" (Copeman, *Singing in Latin* 20).

Table 4: English Latin Pronunciation

Vowels in Accented Syllables				
A	500s		[a]	
	800-1066		[ɑ]	
	1066-1400		[a]	
	1400-1650		[æ]	
		In chant	[æ] or [ɛ]	
	Old Style		[æ]/[e]	I suggest [eI] or [ei] for the second vowel since it is referred to as a diphthong by John Sargeaunt.
AU	1066-1650		[au]	i.e., diphthong
	Old Style		[ɔ]	
E/Æ/Œ	500s		[ɛ]/[e]	
	800-1066		[ɛ]	Not a very open sound, tending toward [e]
			[æ]	For Æ and Œ, also possible in this period
	1066-1400		[e]	ER was [ar] or [ær], e.g., *persona*

	1400-1650	In the earlier part of this period	[ε]	
		In the mid to later part	[i] or [e]	
		In chant	[i]	
		For Œ only	[e]	
	Old Style		[ε]/[i]	
		For Æ only	[i]	

I/Y *(for consonantal I/J see under "Consonants" below)*

	500s		[I]/[i]	
	800-1066		[I]	
	1066-1400		[I]/[i]	
	1400-1650		[əI]	
	Old Style		[I]/[ai]; or [ʌi] (in open syllables)	
		Final I was	[ai]	
O	500s		[o]	
	800-1066		[ɔ]/[ou]	
	1066-1400		[ɔ]/[u]	
	1400-1650		[ɔ]	
	Old Style		[ɒ] /[ou], or [ɔ]/[o]	
U	500s		[ʊ]/[u]	

	800-1066		[u]	With lips protruded, tending toward [y]
	1066-1400		[ʊ]/[y]	With a slight glide, probably [jy]
	1400-1650		[u]/[u] or [y] or [Y]	With a slight glide, probably [jy], except after R or consonantal I/J where the sound was [u]
		In chant	[ə] in endings of –US and –UM with [ʌ] being used more frequently toward the latter part of this period	
		Old Style	[ʌ]/[ju], but [u] after [r], [dz], or [tʃ]. Also possible: [ʊ]/[Y]	
Vowels in Unaccented Syllables				
A	500s		[a]	
	800-1066		[ə] or [a]	
	1066-1400		[a]	AU was [au]

	1400-1650		[a], but Rigg suggests [æ] by the 1600s	
		In chant	[ə]/[ɛ]	AU was either [ɔ] or [au].
	Old Style		[a]	
		In final position, possibly	[ei]	
E/Æ/Œ	500s		[ɛ]	
	800-1066		[ɛ]/[e] tending toward [i]	(same as for Accented above)
		For Æ and Œ, possibly	[æ]	
	1066-1400		[e] or [I]	ER was [ɛr]. *Celis* was either [sɛlis] or [sɛllIs]
	1400-1650		[ə] or [ɛ]/[i] or [ɛ]/[I]	EI was pronounced [i] in some repertoire. Final –ES was [iz] by the 1600s. Final –ER was [ər].
	Old Style		[i]	
I/Y	500s		[I]	
	800-1066		Rigg suggests: [I].	Copeman suggests following

				pronunciation rules as in German.
		Final –IS	[Is]	
	1066-1400		[I]	
	1400-1650		[I]	Ending –IS was always [Is]
	Old Style		[I]	
O	500s		[ɔ]	
	800-1066		Rigg suggests: [ɔ].	Copeman suggests following pronunciation rules as in German.
	1066-1400		[ɔ]	
	1400-1650		[ɔ]	Final –OS was either [ɔs] or [əs] except *cælos* which was pronounced with [o].
	Old Style		[ɔ], [ow], or [oʊ]	
U	500s		[ʊ]/[Y]	
	800-1066		Rigg suggests: [ʊ]/[Y].	Copeman suggests following pronunciation rules as in German.
	1066-1400		[ʊ]/[Y]	

	Old Style		[ʊ]/[ju]; or [Y] in open syllables	

Consonants

C

-Rigg provides a general rule:

	Until 1200	Before front vowels	[ts]	As in Norman French
	After 1200	Before front vowels	[s]	e.g., *cædo* = [sɛdo]

-Copeman suggests:

	All eras	Before a back vowel or before R and L, and in final position	[k]	e.g., *cresco* = [krɛsko]
	800-1066	Medially between back vowels	[kʰ]	
		As an initial consonant before front vowels and medially after I	[tʃ]	
	1066-1400	Before A	[tʃ]	e.g., *cantare*, which evolved

				into the English word: *chant*
	1400-1700	Before front vowels	[s]	
		Before back vowels or a consonant	[k]	
		Before N, C was sometimes softened to	[g]	e.g., *sancta* = [saŋgta]
	Old Style	Before E or I	[s]	
		In all other positions	[k]	
CI + vowel	Until 1500		[sI]	
	1500-early 1600s		[sj]	
	Early 1600s+		[ʃj]	e.g., *Græcia*
	Old Style		[ʃi]	But CIO may be [ʃio] or [ʃo]
CC		After a back vowel and before a front vowel	[ks]	As in the English words *accident* and *occident*
		In all other positons:		
	800-1066		[ttʃ]	e.g., *ecce* = [ɛt–tʃe]
	1066-early 1200s		[kts]	

	1400-1650 and Old Style		[ks]	e.g., *ecce* = [ɛk–si]
CH (for *michi* and *nichil* see under HI below)				
	1066-1400	Before both front and back vowels	[tʃ]	Latin *caritas* became English *charity*
	1400-1650	Before a vowel	[tʃ]	Latin *Michaël* became English *Mitchell*
		Before a consonant	[k]	
	Otherwise, in all eras		[k]	
CT	1066-1400	Before a front vowel	[si]	
		Otherwise	[t]	
D		Generally	[d]	
		In final position	[t]	English Latin rhymes indicate *Dauid*: *lauit*. Misspellings indicate *nequit* instead of *nequid*, and *set* instead of *sed*.
	1400-1650	When ending any syllable	[ð] or [t]	
DI		Normally as spelled, however, in some words pro- nounced	[dʒ]	e.g., *diabolus*, often spelled *zabolus*, and *diurnalis*, spelled *jornalis*

63

				which became English *journal*
G	Accor-ding to Rigg, in all eras	Before back vowels and consonants R and L	[g]	
	600-800		[j]	Slightly guttural [j] before front vowels
	800-1066	Possibly in all positions	[ç], [j], or [x] or, as follows	
		Before back vowels	[g]	
		Before front vowels	[ʒ]	
	1066-1400	Before front vowels	[dʒ]	
	1400-1650	Before E and sometimes I	[dʒ]	However, *Gilbertus* and *gimel* use [g]
		In all other positions	[g]	
	Old Style	Before E or I	[dʒ]	
		In all other positions	[g]	
GN	800-1066		[ŋgn]	

	1066-1400		[ŋgn], or [ŋn], or even [n]. The same rules apply for GM.	French teachers in England during this time were trying to teach [ɲ], but students may have only been able to pronounce [ŋn].
	1400-1650		[ŋgn]	Although Cambridge reformers were using simple [gn] as an ideal, it was not universally pronounced. Rigg provides [ŋgn] between vowels as a general rule. He cites the English Latin misspellings: "dingnus" and "angnus" for *dignus, agnus*.
H (for *mihi* and *nihil* see under HI below)	600-800	Between vowels	[x]	
	800-1066	In initial position	[h]	
	1066-1400		Mute	Often not pronounced due to Norman influence.

	1400-1650		[h]. Very lightly aspirated between vowels or left out completely. It was considered more tasteful to leave out the H if possible. In *nos homines* one can leave out the H; but pronouncing it in a phrase such as *Confirma hoc Deus*, avoids an undesirable guttural stop. Rigg indicates that H was not pronounced at all in the Medieval and Renaissance eras. He notes that it is often omitted in spelling, as in *ac* (hac) and *abet* (habet), or erroneously added, as in *honus* (instead of correct *onus*).	
	Old Style		[h]	e.g., [dʒɛ–ho–va] for *Jehovah* and [mai–hai] for *mihi*
HI-	1066-1400		A strongly aspirated [h], possibly [ç] or [dʒ]	
	1400-1650	For *Hierusa-lem, Hiericho, Hieronimus*	[dʒ]	Copeman provides no other rules for the pronunciation of HI during

				this period. Rigg suggests to use [dʒ] in names beginning with *hier–*, i.e., *Hierusalem, Hiericho, Hieronimus.*
For *mihi* and *nihil*, and for *michi* and *nichil* (the medieval English Latin spellings)	600-800		[x]	
	800-1066		[ç]	
	1066-1400		a strongly aspirated [h]	
	1400-1650		[tʃ]	
	Old Style Latin		[h]	
I/J before a vowel and between vowels	In all eras		[dʒ]	E.g., *iudex* = [dʒYdɛks], which became English *judicial*, and *eius* = [ɛdʒʊs] according to Rigg. However, Copeman gives [dʒ] only for the years 1066–1650 (he does not list any pronunciation for the years before 1066).

		For the exclamation *eia*:	[j] or [dʒ]	[j] according to Rigg since it is often spelled *eya;* but Copeman advises to use [dʒ] here from 1066–1400.
	1400-1650		[dʒ]	In words *eius* and *eia*, Copeman states to use [edʒʊs] and [edʒa] but suggests [j] in *alleluia*.
	Old Style		[dʒ]	
NCT			[ŋt] or [nt]	[nt] is possible as is seen from the rhyme *ante*: *sancte*.
	800-1066		[ŋg]	This also applies to NG and NQ.
	1066-1400		[ŋkt], [ŋgt], [ŋt], or [nt]	Therefore, *sanctus* could have been pronounced [saŋktʊs], [saŋgtʊs], [saŋtʊs], or [santʊs].
QU	Before 1200		[k]	Due to French influence *qui* would have

				been pronounced [ki].
	After 1200	Before O and U	[k]	The following rhymes give evidence of this: *décor/æquor, decus/æquus, tenebrasco/ cras quo.*
		Before A, E, and I	[kw]	
	800-1400		[kw]	
	1066-1400		[ku]	quu– was [ku].
	1400-1650		[kw]	Except *quo* was pronounced [ko], and *quum* was [kʊm].
R	800-1650		[r]	
	All other eras		[ɾ]	
S				

| | All eras | | [s] | |
| | All eras | Between vowels | [z] | |

	600-800		[s] usually, though possibly [z] between vowels.	
	800-1066	At the beginning and end of words and before unvoiced consonants	[s]	
		Between vowels	[z]	
	1066-1400	Between vowels and voiced consonants	[z]	
	1400-1650	In initial position of a syllable, e.g., compound words: *resurrexi* and *resurgentis*	[s]	
			[z]	Between vowels: Copeman recommends a slightly voiced [z], and advises to use [z] even in liaison, i.e., between words.

			[s] or [z]	In final position after an unstressed vowel, this consonant is uncertain. Although 16th-century English began to use [z] in final position (e.g., *was*, *is*), Rigg cites two ambiguous documentations by Robinson: *decus* with final [z] and *cælos* with final [s].
	Old Style	In final position	[s] or [z]	
SC	800-1066		[ʃ]	Copeman provides examples *scientia* and *suscipe* but does not discuss the pronunciation of SC before a back vowel.
		Before A, O, U, R, and L	[sk]	e.g., *scando* [skando], according to Rigg.

		Before E, Æ, Œ, and I	[s]	As in the loan words: *science*, *disciple*
T	1400-1650	In final position	[Θ] or [t]	Copeman cites the following rhyme, c. 1492: "Unto Marie he that loue hath, To here synge he, '*Magnificat*'" (Ryman qtd. in Copeman, *Singing in Latin, or, Pronunciation Explor'd* 35).
	All other eras		[t]	
TH	1066-1400		[Θ] or [t]	Possibly [t] until early 1300s, due to French influence.
	1400-1650		(See under T above)	
	All other eras		[t]	
TI + vowel	800-1066		[tsi]	
	1066-1400		[sI]; but [stI] in words with –*stio* and *stia*	

	1400-1650		[si]	
	Early 1600		[ʃiɔ] or [ʃɔ] are both possibilities	
V				
- Rigg suggests:				
	All eras		[v]	
- Copeman suggests:				
	800-1066		[v]	Pronounced lightly
		If preceding a consonant	[u]	
	1066-1400		[v]	
	1400-1650		a light [v] closer to [f]	
X			[ks]	
XI	1066-1400		[ksi]	
XT	1066-1400		[st]	
Z	800-1066	In Biblical names	[ts]	
	1066-early 1200s		[dz] or [ts]	
	Early 1200s-Present		[z]	

Old Style English Latin

Swift's rhymes from the 18th century provide us with useful data for the pronunciation at this time: *ecclesiæ*/"please ye," *ad infinitum*/"still to bite 'em," (Copeman, *Singing in Latin, or, Pronunciation Explor'd* 195). It is from this period of pronunciation that modern–day English speakers continue to use English Latin. Medical, legal, and botanical jargon, as well as Latin names, are pronounced in Old Style English Latin, such as *verbatim, ratio, Cæsar, Cicero, habeas corpus, ad hoc, e pluribus unum, vice versa,* and *et cetera.* This pronunciation is appropriate for the music of Blow, Purcell, and Wesley (198).

Although Elizabeth I had a fluent mastery and respect for the Latin language, she mandated that religious services were to be conducted in English.[17] Elizabeth did allow for its use in some college chapels and universities. Furthermore, it is said that she passed an Act which mandated sole use of the English pronunciation of Latin at Westminster School.[18] Therefore, Old Style English Latin has been preserved at this institute through the present day.

Thorough documentation of this pronunciation comes from John Sargeaunt in his *Annals of Westminster School.* He provides five rules for what he calls the "Westminster Pronunciation of Latin." For the most part, this pronunciation continues the same pattern of open and closed vowels being dictated by the open or closed syllable. However, some exceptions will be seen below. A Latin dictionary will be of assistance in the preparation of a text in this style of Latin; yet caution must be used here. Seargeaunt's use of the terms "long" and "short" do not represent Classical sounds, but

---

[17] A well–documented event occurred when Elizabeth I rebuked a disrespectful Polish ambassador in a highly impromptu, yet most eloquent manner in Latin. Elizabeth's court was so highly impressed by her control of the language that this event won her great respect. It was said that her "...'ready utterance' of Latin surpassed most university scholars" (Ascham qtd. in Green).

[18] An interesting anecdote regarding the defiance of this Act in the twentieth century can be found in a letter to the editor of The Times by Henry Lunn in Appendix A.

what in English is referred to as long and short vowels.
Furthermore, simply because a vowel is long or short in a Latin
dictionary does not mean that it will be pronounced long or short as
in English. Sargeaunt's rules and exceptions must still be followed,
since Old Style English Latin will sometimes retain the original
quantities and sometimes not. For clarification, the following IPA
was prepared by me. One can see how the pronunciation of the long
vowel also became the name of the vowel in English.

A: short: [a] or [æ]

long: [ei] or [eɪ]

E: short: [ɛ]

long: [i]

I: short: [ɪ]

long: [ai] or [aɪ]

O: short: [ɔ]

long: [ou] or [oʊ]

U: short: [ə]

long: [ju] or [Y]

Sargeaunt outlines the following rules:[19]

1. All letters of English words derived from Latin are to be
pronounced in the English manner. Therefore, C and G before E and
I sound like S and J respectively, e.g., *civis* and *genus* (273–4). He
further states that a stressed or half–stressed vowel before another
vowel or H is to be pronounced "long," e.g., *deus* [di:–əs] and
Diomedes [daiomədiz]; and that long A, I, and O are diphthongs as
in English (274).

2. Sargeaunt states that all enclitics[20] and monosyllabic
words ending in a consonant, use "short" vowels: *–que, –ve, –ne,*

---

[19] IPA transcriptions are mine.
[20] A morpheme attached to the end of a word and dependent upon it but
with individual meaning. The *–que* in *filioque* means "and," providing the
meaning: "and (from) the son "

que, sol, quin, hæc with the exception of *huic*. All others use "long" vowels, e.g., *me, qui* (274).

3. In disyllabic[21] words, the first vowel, if followed by a single consonant, or TR, is sounded as a long vowel, e.g., *amo* [eimo], *patrem* [peitrɛm]. He cites the following "traditional" exceptions: *ibi, tibi, sibi, quibus, Paris*, and any vowels conjugated from *sum*, including *ego* (of Greek influence). In all others, the first syllable is sounded short, e.g., *cinctus, sanctus* (274).

4. In words of more than two syllables, if the penultimate is a (Classically) long vowel, the vowel should be sounded long if before a single consonant, as in *monebam* and *amavi*. If the penultimate is short, the antepenultimate is also to be sounded short as in *monitum* and *veritus*. However, in previous syllables the traditional Classical quantities are to be observed. If, however, the penultimate vowel (other than U) precedes another vowel, the antepenultimate is pronounced long: *habeo* [heibio], *melior* [milijɔr], *imperium* [Impiriəm]; but *monui* (having a Classically short O in the antepenultimate syllable, and a U in the penultimate) would be pronounced [mɔnuI]. The exception is where the two vowels are both I or its equivalent as in *utilis, Pythius, video* [vIdiou], and *inhibeo* [InhIbiou]. Sargeaunt further states that the same rule applies to earlier vowels: the first syllable of *amaverunt* is short.

5. Exceptions to the above rules are initial prefixes which keep their quantity: *subit* (Copeman clarifies that the syllabification is "sub–it"), *redeo*, and *ineo* (274).

Sargeaunt continues in the final *nota bene* paragraph that in previous years, the fourth rule has not been applied to words ending in dactyl (i.e., long–short–short) or cretic (i.e., long–short–long) rhythms where a long vowel, unless it is followed by two consonants, keeps its quantity, except in proper names. Therefore, *sidera* is [saIdəra], but *Lydia* is [lIdija]. Although the above rules seem complex, the

---

[21] A word with two syllables.

choral conductor will be able to find many Latin words with English Latin transcriptions in IPA in the Oxford English Dictionary.

CHAPTER 6: FRENCH & FRANCO-FLEMISH LATIN

"My dear Saxon, this music is in the French style, of which I have no knowledge."
–Corelli to Handel on playing a French overture (qtd. in Copeman, *Singing in Latin, or, Pronunciation Explor'd* vi)

The pronunciation of the Celtic Gauls of the language of their Roman conquerors was notorious in the Empire (Copeman, "French Latin" 90). Eventually, it was further affected by Germanic tribes from the fifth to the tenth centuries (90). Since French pronunciation of Latin evolved from century to century and region to region, as did the Latin pronunciations in other countries, no one pronunciation of a "French Latin" can be given. Two notable features of French pronunciation can be obtained from Norman England by the twelfth century: that of the C and G. C had been palatalized and sibilized from [k] to [ts] when it preceded the frontal vowels E and I, (e.g., *cælum*), which by the thirteenth century moved even more forward to [s] (90). G before E (and sometimes I) had evolved in pronunciation from [g] to [dʒ] and finally to [ʒ] by the thirteenth century (90).

Nasales

According to Copeman, nasalization in French and French Latin, gradually occurred in vowels before N and M, and then affected A and E when preceeding O, I and U in that order (90). However, some scholars state that vowel nasality already existed in Classical Latin, where final M was elided before a word beginning with a vowel (Allen 80). Final M was even left out in inscriptions (Sampson 49). A third–century B.C. tomb reads: "DUONORO [sic] OPTUMO FUISE VIRO" which in proper Classical Latin should be written "*Bonōrum optimum fuisse virum*" ("to have been the best of good men") (49). Sampson states that, although official inscriptions from the late second century B.C. tend to indicate final M, popular inscriptions in all regions of the Empire and at all periods omit it (49). Although this may indicate the preservation of vowel nasality in French and Portuguese from Classical Latin, Sampson states that this is much debated. However, Roger Woodard in *The Ancient Languages of Europe* maintains that Classical Latin did nasalize vowels. He argues that long I, E, A, O, and U before nasal consonants were nasalized (77). These occurred in word–final positions, e.g., –IM, –EM, –AM, –OM, –UM, and before a nasal followed by a continuant.[22] e.g., –NA, –MO (77). If this is true, it can be argued that French Latin (and Portuguese Latin) preserved vowel nasality — a feature not found in Italian, English, or German pronunciations of Latin.

Syncope and Syllabification

The passage of Latin words into French kept the accent on the correct syllables even with the phenomenon of syncope (Hodgman 549). This led to the characteristic emphasis (or lengthening) of final syllables in French. Where the accented

---

[22] A sound produced where the vocal tract is not fully closed and which can be continued without change to airflow or vocal tract position. This includes all vowels and fricatives.

syllable is the third in Latin, *veredictum* became the French *verdit*, and *ornamentum* became *ornement*. Syncope can be seen in the removal of the final syllable as in the first example, or the transition of the nasalized syllable one syllable over, as in the second example. The phenomenon of syncope also occurs on the penultimate syllable, which moves word stress to the final syllable: *simulare* became *sembler*. A retroactive tendency with the singing and speaking of Latin then occurred where the French tended to emphasize and lengthen the final syllable as in French. Weak consonantal groups (i.e., GN, and L or R when preceded by a consonant other than L or R) belong to the following syllable, e.g., *se–clu–sus, fe–bris*, and *se–cre–tus* (Copeman, *Singing in Latin, or, Pronunciation Explor'd* 207). This also has implications for vowel quality since the vowel will be closed now that an open syllable has been created (i.e., the E in the first syllable of each of the above examples will then be [e]).

The following data come from Copeman *Singing in Latin or Pronunciation Explor'd* 146–147, 155–165, and 206–211, and the same author's chapter, "French Latin," in *Singing Early Music* 95–98. The Franco–Flemish pronunciation is appropriate for Machaut, Binchois, Dufay, Ockeghem, Obrecht, Josquin, Clemens non Papa, Willaert, and Lassus (Copeman, *Singing in Latin, or, Pronunciation Explor'd* 148). In the period from 1650–1900s, double consonants are not doubled, however, the preceding vowel should be opened (Copeman, *Singing in Latin* 210–211).[23]

---

[23] The monks of Solesmes have still retained some French vowel qualities in their singing. Notable features are [aɲjYs] (for *agnus*) in their *Gloria I* (although their *magnam* is Italian [maɲam]), the use of [Y] for U, and the frequent use of [e]. Evidence of this can be found in their 1930 recording, *Gregorian Chant Rediscovered*.

Table 5: French Latin Pronunciations

Vowels				
A	800–1250		[a]	Very forward
	1250–1650		[a]	
	1650–early 1900s		[a]	Very forward
	Early 1900s+		[ɑ]	
AM/AN	800–1250	In Francien Latin	[ãm] and [ãn] respectively	
		Normandy	[ã]	
	1250–1550		[ãm] and [ãn] respectively	
		AM/AN + C, Q, G or P	[am] and [aŋ] respectively	Here, the vowel was denasalized, e.g., *angeli* was [aŋg–], *sanctus* was [saŋt–], etc.
	1550–1650		[ã]	The nasal consonant itself ceased to be pronounced.

	1650–1900s	When followed by the phonemes [k], [g], or [p], when followed by M or N, or when not followed by any other consonant	[am] and [an] respectively	e.g., *namque* = [nam–], *flammam* = [flamam]
		In all other positions	[ãn]	e.g., *ante* = [ãnte]. Copeman states that the nasal consonant may be left out when singing in order not to impede the legato demanded by the vocal line. In *sanctus*, the C was silent until about 1800.
AU	900s+		[o]	
	1250–1650		[ɔu]	Possibly in the north
	1250–1300		[au]	
	1300–1500		[ao]	

	1500–1650		[o]	Sometimes [au] if the composer was influenced by the reforms
	1650–1900s		[o]	
E/Æ/Œ	–800	For E	[eI], developing into [I]	
		For Æ/Œ	[ε]	
	800–1250	In accented open syllables	[ei]	e.g., [deiyz] for Deus
		In final position	[ə] or mute	
		Otherwise	[e]	
	1250–1650		[e]	
	1250–1800		*–des* = [de]; *–tes* = [tε]; *et* was [e] even before a vowel	
			"EX" in compound words was [jœ] ([jœz] in liaison)	As in Fr. *yeux*, e.g., *excelsis* was [jœ–zel–siz]
	1650–1900s		[ε]/[e]	Except *"et"* which was traditionally pronounced [et]. E before a weak

				consonant (e.g., GN, L, and R) may have been more closed (e.g., *Emanuel,* where the second E is [e] even though it is found in a closed syllable).
EM/EN	800–1050		[ɛ̃m] and [ɛ̃n] respectively	
	1050+		[ãm] and [ãn] respectively	
	1250–1800		[ãm] and [ãn] respectively	However, – ENS was [ɛnz]; ENT was [ɛt].
			[en]	In Norman Latin
	1550–1650		[ã]	In Norman Latin
	1800–1900s		[am] and [an] respectively	
		If followed by another consonant	[ɛ̃] with both consonants sounded	e.g., *semper* = [sɛ̃mpɛr]. Copeman advises that the nasal consonant may be left out when singing in order not to

				impede the legato demanded by the vocal line.
Accented ER	1250–1800		[ar]	
		As an ending, was probably	[ɛ]	
		Before a vowel	[ɛr]	
EU	1250–1650		[œ], sometimes [y]	For *Deus*, *meus*, and similar words, see U below
I/Y	Until 800			Often pronounced as E above
	800–1250		[i]	
	1250–1650		[i]	
		In final position, possibly	[ei] or [əi]	
	1650–1900s		[i]	
-IS	1250–1650	At the end of a phrase or before a vowel	[iz]	but before another consonant S is mute.
IM/IN	1250–1650		[ĩ]	Towards 1500 [ɛ̃] was also used.

	1650–1900s	Earlier in the period:	[im] and [in], respectively	
		Later in the period:	[ɛ̃m] and [ɛ̃n], respectively	
		Late 1600s to late 1700s also possible	[ĩm] and [ĩn], respectively	
	Present		[in]	
O	Until 800		[oʊ] developing into [ʊ]	
	800–1250		[ɔ]; [ɔ]/[o]	[ɔ] always in the early centuries; then [ɔ]/[o] by the 1200s
		In the south of France	[ɔ]/[u]	
	1250–1650	In closed syllables (with non–nasal consonant)	[o] or [u]	
		In open syllables	[o]	
	By 1500s		[u]	
	1650–1900s		[o]/[ɔ]	
OM/ON	800–1250		[om] and [on] respectively	

86

	1250–1650		[ũm] and [ũm] respectively	
		In Francien Latin	[õm] and [õn], respectively; but from 1500 was [ɔ̃m] and [ɔ̃n], respectively	
	1650–1900s	Before M and N + consonant other than M or N	[ɔ̃]	e.g., *fons* was [fɔ̃z]
		Where there are two nasal consonants, denasalization occurred and either both consonants were pronounced, or the second only.		e.g., omnes = [ɔmnɛz] or [ɔnnɛz].
U	800	Often pronounced as O above		
	800–1250	In northern France	[Y]	
		In closed syllables, generally	[y]	
		In closed syllables in Norman Latin	[iu]	
		In closed syllables in Francien Latin	[y]	

	1250–1650	In open syllables and in final –US	[y]	Except *Deus* and similar words were [de–œz]. UI was [yi].
	1650–early 1900s	At the end of a word, or before a non–nasal consonant	[y]	e.g., *manu, Dominus*
	1900s		[y], [Y], or [u]	Recordings of the monks of Solesmes reflect the second phoneme
UM/UN	Until 800	Final –UM	either [õm] or [õn]	partly nasalized
	800–1250	possibly	[on]	
	1250–1650	Before a second consonant, possibly	[um] and [un], respectively	
	1250–1400		[ym] and [yn], respectively	
	1400–1550		[ỹm] and [ỹn] respectively	
	1550–1599		[ɔ̃] (for both)	
	1650–1900s	before M, MM, MN and for –*umque*	[om], [ɔm], or [ʌm]	e.g., *cum, autumnus*

	1650-1800	Before M, N + non–nasal consonant	[õ]	e.g., *mundi* = [mõdi]
	After 1800		[ɔ̃]	
–UNC–	After 1800		[œ̃]	e.g., *defunctorum* = [defœ̃torɔm]
Consonants				
BS			[s]	
BT			[t]	
BV			[v]	
C	Until 800	Before E, Æ/Œ, and I	[ts]	
		In Picard and Norman areas	[tʃ]	
	800–1250	Before E, Æ/Œ, and I	[ts]	
		Before A	[tʃ] or [ts]. [k] is a possibility in the latter part of this period	
	1250–1650	Before front vowels	[s]	
		Before N	[g]	
		Otherwise	[k]	
	1650–1900s	Before E, I, Æ/Œ, and Y	[s]	
		Otherwise	[k]	
CC	800–1250		[ks] or [ts]	
	1650–1700s		[s]	
	1700s+		[ks]	

CH	800– 1250	Normandy and probably Picardy	[k]	
		Other regions, as follows:		
		- Before back vowels and consonants	[k]	
		- Before front vowels	[tʃ]	
	1250– 1650	Before front vowels	[ʃ]	
		Otherwise	[k]	
	1650– 1900s	Before a back vowel or a consonant	[k]	
		Otherwise	[ʃ]	
CT			[t]	
D	Until 800	Before I + vowel	[dʒ]	
	1250– 1650		usually [d] but sometimes [t]	e.g., *adveniat* was [atvenia]
DV			[v]	
G	Until 800	Before A, E, or I at the start of a syllable	[dʒ]	
	800– 1250	Before A, E, or I	[dʒ]	
		In Picard and Norman Latins	[g]	
	1250– 1900s	Before front vowels	[ʒ]	
		Otherwise	[g]	

		Before front vowels in Picard Latin	[ʒ]	
GN	Until 800		[n]	
	800– 1250		[ñ] or [n]	
		In Paris	[nn]	e.g., *agnus* was [annyz]
	1250– 1650		[n]	
		For *signum* and *regnum*, use	[gn]	
	1650– 1700s		[ɲ]	
	1700s+		[gn]	
GU + vowel	1650– 1900s			(as QU below)
H	800– 1250			Mute
	1250– 1650	Picard Latin		Mute, but can be heavily aspirated for extra emphasis
I/J	Until 800	Before E or I	[dʒ]	
	800– 1250		[dʒ]	
	1250– 1650	Before front vowels	[ʒ]	
		Otherwise, as follows:		
		- Until 1300	[dʒ]	
		- After 1300	[ʒ]	

L:	1250–1650	In final position		Often silent
		In the eastern provinces of Burgundy and possibly Ardennes	tending toward [r]	
NM	800–1250		[nn]	
QU	800–1250	In Francien	[k]	
		In Normandy	[kw]	
	1250–1650		[k]	
	1650–1900s	• qua = [kwa] • que/que = [kẅe] (I suggest the French glide, as such: [kɥe]) • qui = [kẅi] (I suggest: [kɥi]) • quo = [ko] • quu– = [kum] or [kom]. But *equus* = [ekys]/[ekyz]		
PS	Until 1900s		[s]	
R	800–1650		[r]	
S	Until 800		[z]	
	800–1250	Between vowels and in final position	[z]	From 1200, final S was silent except in liaison.
		Otherwise	[s]	
	1250–1650	In final position and between vowels	[z]	EST was [ɛt]; or [ɛ] if next word begins with a

				consonant (see T)
		In Brittany, between vowels in compounds	[s]	e.g., *resurrexionem*
	1650–1900s	Between vowels and in liaison	[z]	Except in compound words, e.g., *desuper*
		In all other positions, even in final position	[s]	i.e., S is not dropped in final position
SC	800–1250	Before E, Æ/Œ, and I	[ts]	
	1250–1650	Before front vowels	[s]	
		Otherwise	[sk]	
	1650–1900s	Before E, I, Æ/Œ, and Y	[s]	
		Otherwise	[sk]	
T	800–1250	In final position	[d]	
		Otherwise	[t]	
	1300–1650	At the end of a word unless followed by a vowel	Mute	
	1650–1900s	In all positions	[t]	

TH	1250–1650		[t]	Possibly applying to all eras as well
TI+vowel	800–1250		[tsi]	However, when preceded by a sibilant was pronounced as written, e.g., *pestium*
	1250–1650		[s]	
		In *–sti–* and *–xti–*, the TI is:	[ti]	Except in *resurrectionem* where it was often spelled *resurrexionem*. See X below.
	1650–1900s		[si]	
		sti–	[sti]	
		–xti–	[ksti]	
V	1250–1650		[v]	
X	800–1250	In final position	[z]	
			[ks]	
		ex	[ɛz]; except in compound words where it was [ez]	e.g., *exhortor*

	1250–1650	In initial position	[s]	
		Otherwise	[z]	EX followed the same rules as "yeux," e.g., *excelsis* = [œzɛlziz]
	1650–1900s		[ks]	
		EX+vowel	[gz]	
XT	1250–1650		[t]	
Z	800–1250		[dz]	
	1250–1650		[z]; also possible: [dz] or [ds]	
	1650–1900s		[z]	

Table 6: Franco-Flemish Latin Pronunciations from 1250-1650

Vowels			
A		[a]	
	Flemish–Dutch Latin		
	- In accented syllables:	[ɑ]	
	- In unaccented syllables	[ə]	
AM/AN		[ãm], and [ã] or [ãn], respectively	Strangely, this would apply to words where AM or AN are not even in the same syllable, e.g., *laudamus*: [lɔ–dãm–Ys] and *manu*: [mãn–Y].
AU		[ɔ]	
	Possibly in the north	[ɔu]	
E/Æ/Œ		[ɛ]/[e]	
	In the lowlands of Brabant, in open syllables	[ei] or [ej]	
EM/EN		[ẽm] and [ẽn] respectively	This probably would also apply to letters not in the same syllable as in AM/AN above
ER	In the lowlands of Brabant	[ar]	
EU		[œ]	

I/Y		[i] (sometimes [I] in closed syllables); but Y was [i]	
IM/IN		[im] and [in] respectively. However, nasalization began evolving in the 1400s/1500s to [ĩ] or [ẽ].	
O		[ɔ]/[u]	
OM/ON		[ũm] and [ũm], respectively	
U		[Y]	
UM/UN	In northern France/Francien Latin	[Ỹm] and [Ỹn], respectively	
	From 1400	[œ̃m] and [œ̃n], respectively	
	From 1600	[œ̃]	
	For Josquin, Copeman suggests to use	[Ỹm] and [Ỹn], respectively.	
	In Flemish music (e.g., Obrecht)	use [ɒm] for UM.	

Consonants			
C	Before back vowels	[k]	
	Before front vowels		
	- In Picard Latin	[tʃ]	Heavy with slight aspirate
	- In Flemish Latin	[ts] with faint [t]	
CC		Probably [kj] moving to [tj]	
CH	In Picard Latin, if the French cognate has [ʃ], then use	[k]	
	In Picard Latin, if the French cognate has [s], use	[ʃ]	
	Walloon Latin	[tʃ]	
	Flemish Latin	[ç]	
G	Before back vowels	[g]	
	In Flemish Latin, aspirated to	[h] or [x]	
	Before front vowels		
	- In Picard Latin	[ʒ]	
	- In Flemish Latin	[ʒ] or [j]	[j] = voiced [ç]
GN		[xn]	
GU+vowel	1650–1900s: (as QU below).		

H		[xn]	
	Picard Latin	Mute, but can be heavily aspirated for extra emphasis	
	Flemish Latin	Weakly aspirated but can be heavily aspirated for extra emphasis	
I/J	In Picard Latin	[ʒ]	
	In Flemish Latin	[ʒ] or [j]	[j] = voiced [ç]
QU		[k]	
	quu– was	[ku]	
R		[r]	
S	As initial consonant	[ts]	
	Between vowels and in liaison	[z]	Even with initial S following a vowel, e.g., *tu solus altissimus* where both Ss of "*solus*" are sounded [z]
	Final S in Picard and Flemish Latins	[s]	
	est was pronounced	[ɛxt]	
T	Before initial consonant of the next word	Mute	

99

TI+vowel	_–tia_	[tʃia]	
	–tio	[zio]	
	–tione	[ziũn]	
X	Before a vowel in Picard Latin	[z]	
	In all positions in Flemish Latin	[ks]	
XC		[z]	
Z		[z]	
	Flemish Latin	[ts]	

WORKS CITED

Apel, Willi. *Gregorian Chant*. Bloomington: Indiana UP, 1958.
    Print.

Boyd-Bowman, Peter. *From Latin to Romance in Sound Charts*.
    Washington, DC: Georgetown UP, 1980. Print.

Brittain, Frederick. *Latin in Church: The History of Its
    Pronunciation*. Oxford: A. R. Mowbray, 1954. Print.

Citroni, Mario. "The Concept of the Classical and the Canons of
    Model Authors in Roman Literature." *The Classical
    Tradition of Greece and Rome*. Ed. James Porter. Princeton:
    Princeton UP, 2006. 204–234. Print.

Copeman, Harold. *Singing in Latin, or, Pronunciation Explor'd*.
    Oxford: Oxford UP, 1990. Print.

——. "French Latin." McGee, Rigg, and Klausner 90–102. Print.

——. "Italian Latin." McGee, Rigg, and Klausner 212–216. Print.

—— and Vera U. G. Scherr. "German Latin." McGee, Rigg, and
    Klausner 258–270. Print.

Dégert, Antoine. "Ecclesiastical Latin." *The Catholic Encyclopedia*.
    New Advent, n.d. Web. 9 Aug. 2008.

Duffin, Ross W. "National Pronunciations of Latin ca. 1490–1600."
    Journal of Musicology 4.2 (1985–1986): 217–226. Print.

Erasmus, Desiderius. *De recta Latini Græcique sermonis
    pronuntiatione*. Ed. J.K. Sowards. Trans. Maurice Pope.
    Collected Works of Erasmus, Vol. 25. U of Toronto P: 1985.
    Print.

Gibbs, Laura. "Final –M and Nasalized Vowels in Latin."
    Grammatice. Blogger, 10 May 2009. Web. 26 January 2010.

Green, Janet M. "Queen Elizabeth I's Latin Reply to the Polish
    Ambassador." *Sixteenth Century Journal* 31.4 (2000): 987-
    1008. Print.

Hodgman, Arthur. "The Correlation of Latin and French." *Classical
    Journal* 20.9 (1925): 547–553. Print.

Holy See & Congregation of Sacred Rites. *Liber Usualis*. New York:

Desclée Co, 1961. Print.

Incorporated Association of Assistant Masters in Secondary Schools.
The Teaching of Classics. London: The Syndics of the
Cambridge UP, 1961. Print.

McGee, Timothy J., and A. G. Rigg, David N. Klausner, eds.
Singing Early Music. Bloomington: Indiana UP, 1996. Print.

McGuire, Martin R.P. "The Pronunciation of Latin: Its History and
Practical Problems." *Teaching Latin in the Modern World*.
Ed. Martin R. P. McGuire. Washington, DC: U of America P,
1960. Print.

Palmer, L. R. *The Latin Language*. London: Faber and Faber, 1961.
Print.

Papal Blessing. *Youtube*. Google, 9 Mar. 2008. Web. 22 Feb. 2010.

Parrish, Carl. *A Treasury of Early Music*. New York: Norton, 1958.
Print.

Parrish, Carl and Ohl John. *Masterpieces of Music Before 1750*.
New York: Norton, 1951. Print.

Pater Noster with Pope Benedict XVI – 03/11/09. *Youtube*. Google,
11 Mar. 2009. Web.   22 Feb. 2010.

Peck, Harry Thurston. *Latin Pronunciation: A Short Exposition of
the Roman Method*. New York: Henry Holt, 1894. Print.

Pius X, Pope St. "*Tra le sollecitudini*: Letter to the Cardinal Vicar of
Rome." *Adoremus Bulletin*. Adoremus Society for the
Renewal of the Sacred Liturgy, 2005. Web. 10 Feb. 2010.

Ranum, Patricia. *Méthode de la Prononciation Latine Dite Vulgaire
ou a la Francaise*. Arles: Actes Sud, 1991. Print.

Reeves, Anthony R. "The Use of French Latin for Choral Music."
Choral Journal 42.3 (2001): 9–16. Print.

Rigg, A. G. "Anglo–Latin." McGee, Rigg, and Klausner 46–61.
Print.

Sampson, Rodney. *Nasal Vowel Evolution in Romance*. New York:
Oxford UP, 1999. Print.

Sargeaunt, John. *Annals of Westminster School*. London: Methuen
and Co. 1898. Print.

Traupman, John C. *The Bantam New College Latin and English Dictionary*. New York: Bantam Books, 1995. Print.

Woodard, Roger, Ed. *The Ancient Languages of Europe*. Cambridge: Cambridge UP, 2008. Print.

WORKS CONSULTED

Alington, C. A. "The Pronunciation of Latin." *Greece & Rome* 2.4 (1932): 2–4. Print.

Berry, Mary. "Gregorian Chant: The Restoration of the Chant and Seventy–Five Years of Recording." *Early Music* 7.2 (1979): 197–217. Print.

Blaise, Albert. *A Handbook of Christian Latin: Style, Morphology, and Syntax*. Washington, DC: Georgetown UP, 1994. Print.

Davidson, Audrey Ekdahl. "Hildegard of Bingen: The Ordo Virtutum." *Women in Music: Music Through the Ages: Composers Born before 1599*. Eds. Martha Furman Schleifer and Sylvia Glickman. Vol. 1. New York: G.K. Hall, 1996. 51–55. Print.

Dean and Chapter of Westminster. "Guide to the Coronation Service." *Westminster Abbey*. Dean and Chapter of the Collegiate Church of St. Peter Westminster, n.d. Web. 22 Feb. 2010.

Dillon, Janete. *Language and Stage in Medieval and Renaissance England*. New York: Cambridge UP, 1998. Print.

Distler, Paul F. *Teach the Latin, I Pray You*. Chicago: Loyola UP, 1962. Print.

Gosine, C. Jane. "Music Reviews: François Couperin: Sacred Vocal Music." *Early Music* 26.1 (1998): 153–154. Print.

Hartlib, Samuel. *The True and Ready Way to Learn the Latin Tongue* (1654). Menston: The Scolar P, 1971. Print.

Hiley, David. *Western Plainchant*. Oxford: Oxford UP, 1993. Print.

Jeffers, Ron. *Translations and Annotations of Choral Repertoire: Sacred Latin Texts*. Corvallis: Earthsongs, 1988. Print.

Kelly, H. A. "Pronouncing Latin Words in English." *The Classical World* 80.1 (1986): 33–37. Print.

Lejay, Paul. "Classical Latin Literature in the Church." *The Catholic Encyclopedia*. New Advent, n.d. Web. 9 Aug. 2008.

Marrieta, Sister. *Singing the Liturgy*. Milwaukee: Bruce Publishing,

1956. Print.

Morehen, John, ed. *English Choral Practice 1400–1650*. Cambridge: Cambridge UP, 1995. Print.

Newman, Barbara. *St. Hildegard of Bingen: Symphonia*. Ithaca: Cornell UP, 1998. Print.

Nicholson, David. *Singing in God's Ear*. New York: Desclée, 1959. Print.

Pius X, Pope St. *Tra le sollecitudini. Adoremus Bulletin*. Adoremus Society for the Renewal of the Sacred Liturgy, 2005. Web. 10 Feb. 2010.

A Queen Is Crowned. Dir. Castleton Knight. Narr. Sir Laurence Olivier. International Historic Films, 1953. Film.

Stevens, John. *Words and Music in the Middle Ages*. Cambridge: Cambridge UP, 1986. Print.

Strunk, Oliver. *Essays on Music in the Western World*. New York: W.W. Norton, 1974. Print.

Waquet, Françoise. *Latin or the Empire of a Sign*. London: Verso, 2001. Print.

Ward, Ralph L. "Evidence for the Pronunciation of Latin (Continued)." *Classical World* 55.9 (1962): 273–275. Print.

Wray, Alison. "The Sound of Latin in England Before and After the Reformation." *English Choral Practice, 1400–1650*. Ed. John Morehen. New York: Cambridge UP, 1995. Print.

DISCOGRAPHY

Dom Joseph Pothier. *1904 Gregorian Congress: Plainchant and Speeches Recorded in Rome*. Cond. Dom André Mocquereau, et al. Perf. Choir of French Seminarians, et al. Gramophone, 1904

Monks of Solesmes. *Chant Rediscovered: The First Recordings by the Choir of Solesmes in 1930*. Cond. Dom Joseph Gajard. Rec. April 1930. EMI, 1994. CD.

Herreweghe, Philipe. *Faure: Requiem and Franck: Symphony in D Minor*. Perf. La Chappelle Royale, Collegium Vocale Gent, Orchestre des Champs Elysées. Rec. Nov. 2001. Harmonida Mundi, 2002. CD.

Britten, Benjamin. *War Requiem*. Cond. Benjamin Britten. Perf. Bach Choir, Highgate School Boys' Choir, Dietrich Fischer-Dieskau, Galina Vishnevskaya, Peter Pears, Rec. 1963. Decca, 1990. CD.

Sequentia. *Hildegard von Bingen: Ordo Virtutum*. Perf. Cologne Sequentia Ensemble for Medieval Music. RCA, 1998. CD.

APPENDIX A: ANECDOTES AND HISTORICAL DOCUMENTATIONS REGARDING LATIN PRONUNCIATIONS

Erasmus, *De recta Latini Græcique sermonis pronuntiatione* (1528)

Lion: . . . What happened was that I suddenly remembered something. Shall I tell you what?

Bear: Yes, if it will make me laugh, too.

Lion: I shall tell you. Not long ago I happened to be present when the emperor Maximillian was listening to some speeches of welcome. These speeches are usually the expression of custom rather than of feeling. Anyway, one of the speakers was a Frenchman from the province of Maine. I shall not mention his name. I do not want to seem to be pillorying the man when in fact I have no ill feelings towards him. His speech was, I suspect, composed by an Italian. It was not bad Latin, but he spoke it with such a French accent that a number of learned Italians present (some of whom you would recognize if I told you their names) thought he must be speaking French. Anyway, when he reached the end — and he muddled that too, stopping dead in the middle of a word, put off presumably by the laughter of those around him — there was the question of who should reply. Ceremony demand that somebody should, but it had to be impromptu as nobody had expected the Frenchman's speech. Eventually they pushed forward a man from the court, who was a doctor.

Bear: How did you know who he was?

Lion: His hat was covered in white fur. That was the evidence. He began like this: *Cæsarea maghestas pene caudet fidére fos et horationem festram lipenter audifit Cæsarea maiestas bene gaudet videre vos et orationem vestram libenter audifit.* 'His imperial majesty is well–pleased to be visiting you and has heard your speech with pleasure.' And so he went on aspirating everything in such a Germanic way that nobody could have sounded more German if he had been speaking in the vernacular. Even louder laughter greeted him. The next speaker was a Dane, though from his speech you would have taken him for a Scotsman so extraordinarily Scots was his pronunciation. The reply to him was given by a Zeelander. You would have sworn that neither was speaking Latin.

Bear: And the emperor? Did he manage not to laugh?

Lion: He was used to such scenes, and had some familiarity with all the languages. I told the story to support what you said about it being most important for a boy to unlearn the bad habits of his native language.

Dom Cuthbert Butler, *The Vatican Council,* qtd. in Frederick Brittain's *Latin in Church*, regarding Vatican Council I of 1870

Even so, uniformity of pronunciation was not expected at the Council. Reporters, in fact, had been specially trained to record the speeches of ecclesiastics with French, Spanish, and other national pronunciations of Latin. Nor were they trained for nothing, for such pronunciations were freely used. Yet, like Queen Elizabeth and the Polish ambassador, the speakers understood one another. Only once, in fact, does there appear to have been serious difficulty in this respect. This was when the bishop of Poitiers — a zealous Ultramontane, it is interesting to note — was making a lengthy speech in Latin, with a French pronunciation. "Some Italian bishops called out that they could not understand. He repeated a sentence slowly in his best Italian style, and then said: *Gallus sum, et Gallice loquor.*"

Harry Thurston Peck, a professor of Columbia College, in *Latin Pronunciation: A Short Exposition of the Roman Method* (1894)

"It is natural that the Roman system should make its way more rapidly into use in this country than in Europe, not because Americans are more given to experiments, but because here in the United States the inconveniences of having no standard system have been more sharply felt. New England being wholly settled from Old England, long continued the English system of pronouncing Latin. In the Middle States, the Germans and Dutch introduced their own methods; in the South and West, the French pronunciation came in quite frequently; and all over the Union, the Catholic clergy in their schools and colleges have propagated the traditional usage of their Church. Hence a Babel of pronunciations and systems existing and practised [sic] side by side, in a picturesque confusion such as no European country ever knew; and hence the general willingness to accept a single method [i.e., the Classical pronunciation of Latin], especially one that is based upon historic truth" (6).

Letter from Pope St. Pius X to Archbishop Du Bois
TO OUR VENERABLE BROTHER LOUIS ERNEST DU BOIS
ARCHBISHOP OF BOURGES

VENERABLE BROTHER:

Your letter of June 21 last, as well as those which We have received from a large number of pious and distinguished French Catholics, has shown Us to Our great satisfaction that since the promulgation of Our MOTU PROPRIO of November 22, 1903, on Sacred Music, great zeal has been displayed in the different dioceses of France to make the pronunciation of the Latin language approximate more closely to that used in Rome, and that, in consequence, it is sought to perfect, according to the best rules of art, the execution of the Gregorian melodies, brought back by Us to their ancient traditional form. You, yourself, when occupying the Episcopal See of Verdun, entered upon this reform and made some useful and important regulations to insure its success. We learn at the same time with real pleasure that this reform has already spread to a number of places and been successfully introduced into many cathedral churches, seminaries and colleges and even into simple country churches. The question of the pronunciation of Latin is closely bound up with the restoration of the Gregorian Chant, the constant subject of Our thoughts and recommendations from the very beginning of Our Pontificate. The accent and pronunciation of Latin had great influence on the melodic and rhythmic formation of the Gregorian phrase and consequently it is important that these melodies should be rendered in the same manner in which they were artistically conceived at their first beginning. Finally the spread of the Roman pronunciation will have the further advantage as you have already so pertinently said, of consolidating more and more the work of liturgical union in France, a unity to be accomplished by the happy return to Roman liturgy and Gregorian chant. This is why We desire that the movement of return to the Roman pronunciation of Latin should continue with the same zeal and consoling success which has marked its progress hitherto; and for the reasons given above We hope that under your direction and that of the other members of the episcopate this reform may be propagated in all the dioceses of France. As a pledge of heavenly favors to you, Venerable Brother, to your diocesans, and to all those who have addressed petitions to Us in the same tenor as your own, We grant the Apostolic Benediction.

From the Vatican, July 10, 1912.

PIUS PP. X

Letter to the Editor of *The Times*, 29 Jan. 1938
WESTMINSTER SCHOLARS – TO THE EDITOR OF THE TIMES

Sir, –

When my third son took his scholarship at Westminster, I was told that the boys used the English pronunciation for Latin because of an Act of Parliament in the reign of Queen Elizabeth.

The Act said: "The boys of St. Peter's College, Westminster, shall speak Latin as the English is spoke, that they may not understand the blasphemous teaching of the Mass". This may be a legend, but it is a fact that the Westminster Scholars who had seats at the Coronation of King George V were instructed to cry at the moment of crowning "Vivat Georgius Rex" and "Vivat Maria Regina", but Queen Mary objected to the English pronunciation of "Maria" and that one word defied the Act of Queen Elizabeth, and was duly pronounced as Romans would have had it done.

Yours faithfully,
HENRY S. LUNN, Reform Club

Letter to the Editor of *The Times*, 29 Jan. 1938

PRONUNCIATION OF LATIN – TO THE EDITOR OF THE
TIMES

As a naval officer whose classical education came to an
abrupt halt at the age of 15 I never ceased to be grateful that I was
taught to pronounce Latin in the old–fashioned way. To those who
have carried their studies sufficiently far to appreciate the rhythm
and beauty of classical literature pronunciation is another matter, but
to the ordinary Englishman the value of such Latin as he acquires by
the age of 15 is that his pronunciation corresponds with that of the
English words derived from it. Such knowledge is invaluable in
picking up a smattering of Spanish, Italian, and other languages in
one's wanderings around the world. Also, such knowledge enables
one to appreciate an occasional Latin quotation. The continuance of
the use of "fancy" pronunciations must be gradually to confine
knowledge and pronunciation of Latin to that minority who complete
their classical studies before they take part in practical affairs or who
enter the learned professions.

– ENGINEER REAR–ADMIRAL W. SCOTT HILL. (Retd.), 40,
Broadway, Westminster, S.W.1.

Letter to the Editor of *The Times*, 29 Jan. 1938

Sir, –

The arguments already advanced in your columns in favor of
the traditional English pronunciation of Latin are sufficiently
convincing.

But there is another, which is perhaps vital. The British are,
in the vast majority, notoriously poor linguists, and this applies
particularly to the so–called Latin languages. Their efforts, when
they dare open their mouths, to pronounce French, for example, are
apt to evoke either pity or merriment. Also, one Esperanto is
enough.

Yours faithfully,

RANDAL NEALE (Chief of Editorial Staff). Reuters, Limited, 9,
Carmelite Street, Thames Embankment, E.C.4.

Responses to the article "Singing in Latin" from *Music & Letters* 32.3 (July 1951): 302–303

Sir,

With more than ordinary appreciation I read your article championing the classical pronunciation of Latin. It is a subject on which I, for one, feel most deeply. Some years ago I was converted to what we think of as the Old Faith; but on those occasions when (say) the Creed is sung by the faithful you will hear one solitary Vergilian devotee proclaiming his belief in "factorem coeli et terræ" as kylee et terri, and on other occasions (as at Christmas) remembering that "gestant Puellæ viscera" is properly rendered with a hard G and NOT that horrid emasculated "vishera–" but a bold "weeskera". On my conversion I asked the good Franciscans whether I might be allowed to be faithful to Vergil & Co., and the reply was: "Heavens, yes! We get all kinds here!" Talking of the difficulties of translation, there are two versions of St. Thomas Aquinas's lovely "Adoro Te devote, latens Deitas" in English. One is to my mind a perfect and sublime pattern of the original; the other is mauled. Yet such is our careless prodigality that both are in use.
– Feltham. GEOFFREY JAGGARD.

Sir,

The lament over a debased Latin pronunciation with Italian "cheesing and chawing" seems to express a state of mind all too prevalent today. Two facts are ignored: first, the words of the Mass are not an isolated aesthetic exercise but part of the worship of the Catholic Church; and secondly the Latin used in the Church's liturgy is itself "debased" in comparison with classical Latin. Yet it is not suggested that the Church's living Latin should be edited to conform to classical purity. I submit that it is as unreasonable to insist on classical pronunciation as to expect the vocabulary and grammar of ecclesiastical Latin to be acceptable to a student of Cicero. The Church, in conformity with the wishes of Pope Pius X, adopts the Roman style of pronunciation; and I question the validity of an apparently arbitrary change from the style of pronunciation universal wherever the liturgy is sung.
– Southborough. F. COULTHARD.

Sir,

It is greatly to be hoped that none of our musical societies will be moved to abandon the "Italian" pronunciation in favour of the "classical". Whatever the merits are of teaching Latin in what is thought to be the pronunciation of the elite of the Golden Age there is no case at all for so pronouncing the words of the Mass, which is essentially a thing of the people and has no connection with Cicero and the rest of them. Latin was not used in the Christian Church until it had become the language of the common people; and this plebeian Latin has been retained by the Church, while in the streets it has grown into Italian, the same principles of pronunciation being common to both.

– Ipswich. H. GRANT SCARFE

APPENDIX B: HISTORICAL TREATISES OF LATIN PRONUNCIATION VARIANTS
(listed in chronological order)

1512–1641: William Lilly. *An English Grammar* or *Lillie's Grammar* (England).

1517: Andreas Ornithoparcus. *Musice active micrologus* (Germany) Trans. John Dowland in 1609 in England as *Andreas Ornithoparcvs: His Micrologus*.

1528: Desiderius Erasmus. *De recta Latini Græcique sermonis pronuntiatione.*

1528 and 1536: Gilles du Guez. *An Introductorie for to lerne, to rede, to pronounce and to speake frenche, trewly compiled for the ryghte hygh, excellent and most vertuous lady, the lady Mary of England doughter of our moste gracious soveraine lorde kyng Henry the eyhte* (England).

1529: Geofroy Tory. *Champ fleury* (France).

1530: John Palsgrave. *Les clarcissement* (Written in England but concerning French).

1555: John Cheeke. *De pronuntiantæ Græcæ potissimum linguæ disputationes* (Written in Basle in 1542).

1559–1560: Pierre (de) la Ramée, AKA Ramus. *Scholæ grammaticæ* (France). Published in English in 1585 as *Latine Grammar*.

1568: Thomas Smith. *De recta & emendata linguæ græcæ pronuntiante* (Written in England).

1568: Thomas Smith. *De recta & emendata linguæ Anglicæ scriptione, dialogus* (Written in England).

1569: John Hart. *An Orthography* (Written in England in 1551).

1573: John Baret. *An Alvearie or Triple Dictionarie in Englishe, Latin, and French* (England).

1580: William Bullokar. *Book at large* (England).

1582: Hercules Castilliard. *Brief advertissement touchant la prononciation latine d'aucuns mots.* Found in Frederick Brittain's *Latin in Church* (88) (Written in France).

1586: Justus Lipsius. *De recta pronunciatione latinæ linguæ dialogus* (Published in Netherlands).

1611: Thomas Coryat(e). *Coryats crudities hastily gobled vp in five moneths trauells in France, Sauoy etc* (England).

1617: Robert Robinson. *The Art of Pronuntiation* (England).

1649: Christoph Bernhard. *Von der Singe–Kunst ode Manier* (Germany).

1653: John Wallis. *Grammatica Linguæ Anglicanæ* (England).

1719 and 1750: Pipoulain–Delaunay. *Alphabet pour les enfants* (France).

1761: L'abbé Moules. *Règles pour la prononciation des langes française et latine* (France).

1798: John Walker. *A Key to the Classical Pronunciation of Greek and Latin Proper Names* (England).

1868: W. Corssen. *Über Aussprach, Vokalismus und Betonung der Lateinischenn Sprache* (Germany).

1871: Henry John Roby. *A Grammar of the Latin Language* (England).

1907: J. P. Postgate. *How to pronounce Latin* (England).

1933: P. Damas. "La prononciation du latin avant la reforme du XVIe siècle." *Revue du chant grégorien*. May–June. 71–82.

1943: J. Marouzeau. *La prononciation du latin* (France).